"In *Broken Cisterns*, Sara [...] many times to groups of wo[...] pages represent more than the fruit of faithful Bible study. They also clearly draw from much personal experience in seeking to turn away from broken cisterns to the living waters found only in Jesus Christ and walking with other women seeking to do the same. The result is a valuable guide for women experiencing spiritual thirst in today's world that is honest, hopeful, biblical, and practical. It will be a helpful resource not only for personal study but also for use in discipleship relationships, women's small groups, or wherever women are seeking to learn and grow together in Christ."

—Dave Baxter, pastor of congregational life,
Christ Covenant Church, Matthews, North Carolina

"Pleasure, success, reputation—they never deliver the satisfaction they promise. That's because God has designed us for something infinitely better—abundant life in His Son. Ivill illuminates what tempts us to wallow in broken cisterns and then shows us biblically and practically how to avoid those pitfalls and live life to the full in Christ our Savior. A terrific read for individuals and book groups!"

—Lydia Brownback, author, Flourish Bible Study series

"We are all looking to have our hearts filled, but often we drink from the sludgy water of broken cisterns instead of from clear, clean springs. Sarah Ivill writes *Broken Cisterns* with insight into the Scriptures and women's hearts. You will see the mud of your heart on the pages of this book, but even more you will see the Living Waters that can make you clean and quench your thirst eternally. With questions to help you examine your life, *Broken Cisterns* is ideal for reading and discussing with a friend."

—Keri Folmar, author of *The Good Portion: Scripture* and
the Delighting in the Word Bible Study series.

"We all have thirsty hearts and seek to quench that thirst through the murky, stagnant cisterns of this world. But Jesus offers more. He offers the living water that truly satisfies. In *Broken Cisterns*, Sarah Ivill helps us see how our hearts are prone to wander, prone to fill our thirst with shallow counterfeits. She then points us to Christ, who meets all the longings of our hearts. For all those who thirst, *Broken Cisterns* will lead you to the well that never runs dry."

—Christina Fox, counselor, writer, speaker, and author
of several books, including *Idols of a Mother's Heart.*

"'How does Sarah know me so well?' This is the question I kept asking as I read *Broken Cisterns*. Sarah understands me and my heart. Many people write about problems, but not everyone has the insight into how to apply the Word to solutions on growing and changing. Sarah does. Sarah pulled me into the great love story of the Bible. She is concrete and never left me wondering about how to live out a deeper, more trusting love for God. Her questions at the end of each chapter are an added plus for personal and group study."

—Helen Holbrook, children's director,
Christ Evangelical Presbyterian Church (PCA)

"God has truly gifted Sarah Ivill to reach deep into the hearts of women. Sarah meets us where we are—in our brokenness, drinking from broken cisterns—and takes us on a journey to find springs of living water. I hope many women will take the opportunity to read her book and learn from it, as I have."

—Jeany Jun, New Life Presbyterian Church
of Orange County

Broken Cisterns

Broken Cisterns

Thirsting for the Creator Instead of the Created

Sarah Ivill

Reformation Heritage Books
Grand Rapids, Michigan

Broken Cisterns
© 2020 by Sarah Ivill

Reformation Heritage Books
2965 Leonard St. NE
Grand Rapids, MI 49525
616-977-0889
orders@heritagebooks.org
www.heritagebooks.org

Scripture taken from the New King James Version®. Copyright © 1982 by Thomas Nelson. Used by permission. All rights reserved.

Printed in the United States of America
20 21 22 23 24 25/10 9 8 7 6 5 4 3 2 1

Library of Congress Cataloging-in-Publication Data

Names: Ivill, Sarah, author.
Title: Broken cisterns : thirsting for the creator instead of the
    created / Sarah Ivill.
Description: Grand Rapids, Michigan : Reformation Heritage Books,
    2020. | Includes bibliographical references.
Identifiers: LCCN 2020024191 (print) | LCCN 2020024192 (ebook) |
    ISBN 9781601787828 (paperback) | ISBN 9781601787835 (epub)
Subjects: LCSH: Christian women—Religious life. | Spirituality—
    Christianity. | Satisfaction—Religious aspects—Christianity.
Classification: LCC BV4527 .I94 2020 (print) | LCC BV4527 (ebook)
    | DDC 248.8/43—dc23
LC record available at https://lccn.loc.gov/2020024191
LC ebook record available at https://lccn.loc.gov/2020024192

For additional Reformed literature, request a free book list from Reformation Heritage Books at the above regular or email address.

To the Fountain of living waters,

*And to all those who have hewed out cisterns for yourselves
and found them to be broken,
may you know the joy of returning to Christ.*

"But My people have changed their Glory
For what does not profit.
Be astonished, O heavens, at this,
And be horribly afraid;
Be very desolate," says the LORD.
"For My people have committed two evils:
They have forsaken Me, the fountain of living waters,
And hewn themselves cisterns—broken cisterns
that can hold no water."

—JEREMIAH 2:11–13

Contents

A Note from Sarah

The outline of this book came from a speaking engagement topic I have shared many times with different groups of women over the past several years, originally titled "Thirsting for Springs of Living Water." Due to the response I received, I decided to expand it into a book, and I am grateful Reformation Heritage Books opened the opportunity to do so. It is my hope that you will study these chapters and discuss the questions in the context of the local church. Hopefully older women will study it with younger women, or mothers will study it with their daughters. It can also be beneficial to read on your own or with a friend and discuss the questions with them sometime during the week.

If you choose to use it for a book study at your church, I encourage you to have the women read the chapter during the week and answer the questions so they can be prepared to discuss them in a group setting. The leader can summarize the chapter and then facilitate the questions. Adding a time of prayer and fellowship around food would be an added blessing. My prayer for those of you doing this study is that you will drink of the water that Christ offers you so that you will never be thirsty again (John 4:14).

Soli Deo gloria!

Acknowledgments

I am grateful for those who have been part of this writing project.

Thank you to Reformation Heritage Books, especially Jay Collier for your support and encouragement of this book, to Donna Huisjen for her editorial skill, and to Annette Gysen and Dr. Joel Beeke for reviewing the manuscript.

Thank you to all the ladies who gave me encouraging feedback at retreats and conferences on this material, which encouraged me to expand it into book form.

Thank you to Lisa Menchinger and Amanda Verret for reviewing an early form of the manuscript and providing encouragement, as well as comments and suggestions.

Thank you to the pastors of Christ Covenant Church (PCA) for faithfully proclaiming the Word of God each week, as well as to the women's Bible study team and the women in my Bible study class, who have faithfully prayed for me and encouraged me.

Thank you to my dad and mom, David and Judy Gelaude, who have always supported me in my love of the Word and encouraged me to do what the Lord has called me to do. I love you both more than words can express.

Thank you to my husband, Charles, and to our children, Caleb, Hannah, Daniel, and Lydia, for your faithful support, encouragement, and prayers.

Finally, thank you to my heavenly Father, to my Lord and Savior Jesus Christ, and to the Holy Spirit. To the triune God for what He has done through me, a broken vessel that too easily and often delights in broken cisterns, yet one that is being renewed in knowledge after the image of the Creator to the praise of His glorious grace.

Introduction

Carol pulled out her iPhone. What started out as an occasional look at social media had turned into a habit that had gotten out of hand. She kept trying to convince herself that she had technology use under control, but she couldn't ignore the countless hours she seemed to lose each week on her phone, how depressed it made her feel when she compared herself to others and their accomplishments, and how empty it left her feeling relationally. What she had thought would enhance her social relationships had turned out to empty her.

Sarah stepped off the scale. When did she get so obsessed with how much she weighed? Counting calories and exercising had become so important they were taking over much of her thought life. What she had thought was a health kick had turned into an addiction to thinness and fitness. What she had thought would fulfill her had failed her.

Gina pulled into the mall parking lot. How long had she been attempting to drown out her problems with shopping? She kept adding more and more debt to her credit card. What she had thought would fulfill her was draining her.

Amy laid her head on the pillow. When did she get hooked on sexual sin? What started out as an irregular occurrence had turned into a deep thirst for more, but she couldn't ignore the emptiness and shame she felt inside. What she had thought would fulfill her had devastated her.

Lisa looked at her calendar. When did she ever stop running here and there and everywhere? She was beginning to realize that her busyness was really her way of ignoring the loneliness she felt inside. What she had thought would distract her had depleted her.

Kay looked at her office wall. So many signs of achievement surrounded her, yet she felt more anxious than ever. She was always looking to meet the next deadline, always hoping she would measure up, always fearing failure. What she had thought would lead to prestige and popularity left her feeling even more insecure.

Tammy looked at her children. She had thought motherhood would make her happy. But after hours of sitting in carpool lines, shopping for the latest designer clothing, sitting on the sidelines cheering them on in their games, and trying to steer them in the right career directions, she realized she had poured so much into them that she hadn't taken time to do much else. She had elevated her role of motherhood so much that she had neglected other important priorities and relationships, especially her relationship with the Lord. What she had thought would fulfill her had frazzled her.

Perhaps you, like me, can relate to one of these women. What they are doing is not new. It's as old as what Eve did in the garden and what Israel did in the wilderness and the promised land. Ponder the Lord's word through Jeremiah:

> "For My people have committed two evils:
> They have forsaken Me, the fountain of
>   living waters,
> And hewn themselves cisterns—broken
>   cisterns that can hold no water."
> (Jer. 2:13)

In Jeremiah's day there were three sources from which Israel could obtain water. First, they could have fresh spring water. This was the best of the best. Think of the best water you've ever tasted from a bottle. However good you thought it was, it would pale in comparison to the fresh running water found in Palestine. Second, Israel could have had well water. This wasn't terrible, but it wasn't the best either. Think about coming in from a hot day and drinking a glass of water that had been sitting on the counter all day. Certainly water, even when it's room temperature, will do when you're thirsty, but it's not nearly as refreshing as a cool glass of water from the refrigerator.

Finally, Israel could obtain runoff water that had collected in a cistern. This was a pit cut into the limestone and then plastered to prevent water from leaking. These cisterns could also collect sediment and mosquito larvae. The only thing worse than drinking a cistern's water would have been trying to drink from a broken cistern. In a broken cistern no water would remain at all, only silt and larvae.[1] I don't know any woman who would put a water bottle up to her mouth and chug down silt and larvae, and yet figuratively many of us are doing just that. We are hewing out cisterns for ourselves, broken cisterns that can hold no water. Understanding why we do this and the danger of doing this will help us say no the next time the world, our flesh, or the devil offers us a broken cistern.

---

1. Paul R. House, "Jeremiah," in the ESV Study Bible: English Standard Version (Wheaton, Ill.: Crossway, 2008), 1372.

Part 1

Broken Cisterns
Lead To…

Chapter 1

An Imperfect World

It was a hot summer Saturday, and my husband and I had decided to take our four children to four different places after having lunch at home. We committed to keeping the final two destinations a surprise. We had a return to make at Staples and we needed an item at Home Depot, so these were our first two nonsurprise stops. We were hoping to get in and out of each store relatively quickly so we could move on to the better surprises, but our younger two children didn't want to stop playing with the pens at Staples and pretending to be employees by taking things off certain shelves to "restock" them. Finally, we managed to get out of Staples and moved on to Home Depot. But we only exchanged pens for lawn mowers. Our children clearly weren't in a hurry. As I sat and watched my four-year-old and two-year-old happily playing and taking their time enjoying the air conditioning and different environments of these places, it suddenly occurred to me that they had no idea of the better surprises ahead. What my husband and I knew was coming (a stop for ice cream and then playing at a splash pad in their bathing suits) wasn't anywhere on their radar. So they settled for pens and lawn mowers.

Isn't that how it is for you and me? We have the glorious riches of God's grace at our disposal, and yet we often content ourselves with the broken cisterns of this world.

We constantly hew out cisterns for ourselves when we have the Fountain of living waters, the Lord God, offering us Himself, His word, His peace, His promises, and His protection.

We Are Worshipers

Eve (along with Adam) had been created in the image of God (Gen. 1:27–28). This means she had been created to reflect His knowledge, righteousness, and holiness and to have dominion over the creatures.[1] Adam and Eve were also given a charge by God: "Then God blessed them, and God said to them, 'Be fruitful and multiply; fill the earth and subdue it; have dominion over the fish of the sea, over the birds of the air, and over every living thing that moves on the earth'" (Gen. 1:28). This charge, also known as the cultural mandate, involved worship, work, woman, and the words of God. Eve was to worship God alone. She was to work for His glory and according to His standards. She was to serve her husband, submitting to his headship and humbly helping him however she could. And she was to look to God's words as her sole authority for all of life. The facts that she was created

---

1. Westminster Shorter Catechism, 10. See Gen. 1:27–28; Col. 3:10; Eph. 4:24.

in the image of God and that God had given her a specific purpose are important for us to realize because they reveal something about all of our hearts.

First, they reveal that we are worshipers. You and I were born to worship. The question, then, is not whether we will worship but who or what we will worship. We know we are to worship God and to glorify and enjoy Him forever, but because of the fall we often fall prey to the temptation from the world, the devil, and our own flesh to worship someone or something other than the one living and true God.

This is what happened to Gina, whom we met in our introduction. The shopping mall had become a shrine. She worshiped materialism instead of her Maker. This happens to you and me too. To whatever we give most of our time, talents, and treasure is what we worship. Scripture says that we must worship God alone: "You shall have no other gods before Me" (Ex. 20:3). Why? Because "I am the LORD your God, who brought you out of the land of Egypt, out of the house of bondage" (Ex. 20:2). Since the Lord has delivered us from slavery to sin, death, and Satan, we are to worship Him alone. Since He alone is King, the psalmists call us again and again to worship Him.

> Oh come, let us worship and bow down;
> Let us kneel before the LORD our Maker.
> For He is our God,
> And we are the people of His pasture,
> And the sheep of His hand. (Ps. 95:6–7)

And "Oh, worship the LORD in the beauty of holiness! Tremble before Him, all the earth" (Ps. 96:9).

When we come to the New Testament, we learn that worship is spiritual, and nothing is to be withheld from the God who has called us each by name. After spending the first nine chapters in his letter to the Romans declaring the great doctrines of the Christian faith, Paul turns to the Christian's duty in Romans 12: "I beseech you therefore, brethren, by the mercies of God, that you present your bodies a living sacrifice, holy, acceptable to God, which is your reasonable service. And do not be conformed to this world, but be transformed by the renewing of your mind, that you may prove what is that good and acceptable and perfect will of God" (Rom. 12:1–2).

In the Old Testament God's people had to sacrifice their best animals on the altar before God in order to atone for their sins and be in good standing with Him. As New Testament believers, we are called to sacrifice ourselves, not to atone for our sins to be in good standing with God (Christ has done that on our behalf), but as our thanksgiving offering for the salvation He has already provided for us. A living sacrifice is far harder to offer than a dead one! The animals used in the Old Testament sacrificial system couldn't crawl back off the altar. But you and I can! Have you ever given your day to Christ, only to take it back again, using your time, talents, and treasures for your own good and glory instead of His? The Lord is asking us to stay on the altar, continually offering our actions, attitudes, accolades, and aptitudes to Him. He doesn't want part of us; He wants all of us.

He wants us to wonder at His glory and His grace (Psalm 29). He wants our mouths open wide in praise of who He is and all He has done (Psalm 150). He wants us to rid our lives of other gods that we bow to each and every day, such as anger, beauty, career, relationships, social media, and sexual sins (Col. 3:5). He wants us to sing gospel songs of grace in our hearts to Him and to each other (Col. 3:16). He wants us to strive for holiness in our lives by His enabling grace (Heb. 12:14). He wants us to invest in kingdom work, leading others to worship Him (Matt. 28:18–20). And He wants us to continually praise Him with the fruit of our lips (Heb. 13:15).

We Are Workers
Second, Genesis 1:27–28 reveals that we are workers. You and I were made to work. The question, then, is not whether we will work but for whom or what we will work. We are to work for the glory of God. "And whatever you do, do it heartily, as to the Lord and not to men, knowing that from the Lord you will receive the reward of the inheritance; for you serve the Lord Christ" (Col. 3:23–24).

But because of the fall, we often work for the glory of people, desiring power, position, possessions, and prestige for our own glory. This is what happened to Kay, whom we also met in the introduction. She had worked for accolades instead of the Almighty. This also happens to you and me. There's a startling contrast in the book of Acts between a couple who worked for their own glory and a couple who worked for God's glory. Ananias and Sapphira sold one of their possessions (a piece of land), but instead of giving all the proceeds to the work of the Lord they kept some of the money for themselves. The sin was not in keeping some of the proceeds. The sin was in lying, in saying they were giving all the proceeds when they really were withholding some of the profit for themselves. Such deceit cost them their lives (Acts 5:1–11).

In contrast, Aquila and Priscilla worked for the Lord. They were tentmakers, just like Paul. In fact, he worked alongside them for a time in Corinth, before they traveled together to Ephesus. Paul continued on to Jerusalem, but Aquila and Priscilla stayed in Ephesus. During their time there they had the opportunity to disciple a young man who was already educated in the Scriptures and fervent for the faith but who needed more accurate instruction. Because of Aquila and Priscilla's fruitful and effective work for the gospel, Apollos went on to minister in another region, publicly and vigorously refuting the Jews and teaching Christ in all of Scripture (see Acts 18). Our work matters; it will either aid in the further proclamation of the gospel or detract from it. May each of us "take heed to the ministry which you have received in the Lord, that you may fulfill it" (Col. 4:17).

The final chapter of Proverbs paints a picture of a wise woman who glorifies God. "She seeks wool and flax, and willingly works with her hands.... She...provides food for her household,... considers a field and buys it.... She girds herself with strength,... perceives that her merchandise is good,... stretches out her hands to the distaff,... extends her hand to the poor,... makes tapestry for herself.... She makes linen garments and sells them,... watches over the ways of her household, and does not eat the bread of idleness.... Give her of the fruit of her hands, and let her own works praise her in the gates" (Prov. 31:13–31). A woman who works for the glory of God will seek the welfare of others. She will willingly work, as to the Lord. She will provide for others' needs. She will consider her work in light of God's wisdom. She will strengthen her arms for service. She will take care of herself, as she is able, so as not to be a burden to others. She will work hard, not in futility but in the fear of the Lord.

In contrast, the unwise woman is also pictured in Proverbs. Most often the unwise woman is pictured as an adulteress (7:5–27; 9:13–18) or as a quarrelsome wife (21:9, 19). She works hard to cause others to wander from truth. Far from seeking the welfare of others, she seeks to trap others by her alluring speech and conduct. Instead of providing for others' needs, she places them in desperate need of rescue from sin. Far from serving, she seduces. Far from loving and working for God, she loves and works for evil. We can be certain that, apart from God's enabling power in our lives, our work will be for our flesh, the world, and the devil.

We Are Wired for Relationships
Third, Genesis 1:27–28 reveals that we were created to live in community with others. God, after declaring all of creation very good, said that it was not good for man to be alone and made a helper for him, Eve (Gen. 2:18). The question, then, is not whether we will be involved

in relationships but how we will honor God in our relationships. We are to be life-givers to those around us, extending a helping hand, lending a listening ear, walking the extra mile with those in need, and sharing our hearts with others (see, for example, Col. 3:12–17). But often we retreat into isolationism and individualism, taking life from others by closing our hands, stopping our ears, running away on our feet, and encasing our hearts.

This is what happened to Lisa, another woman we met in the introduction. She was running from her loneliness, filling her calendar with busyness so that she wouldn't have to face her fear of being alone. It's also what happened to Tammy. She had elevated her relationship with her children to such a degree that she had neglected other necessary relationships, especially her relationship with the Lord. This happens to you and me too. Too often we isolate ourselves in our sin and shame, our suffering, or even in our service. We are good at rugged individualism, thinking we can manage things on our own. But according to Scripture, this is not God's way.

The picture that Paul paints in Ephesians of believers living in right relationships is instructive for us. We are to walk in both unity (4:1–16) and purity (4:17–5:17). We must recognize that we need each other, especially each other's gifts that Christ has given to us, as well as each other's love that flows from God's love for us, in order to run this race of grace for God's glory. When we withdraw from our sisters, we withhold from them an important part of the body. Regardless of whether you are a hand or a toe, you're needed! For example, an older woman in the church may have studied the Bible all her life. She may think she doesn't need to come to Bible study anymore. But she's forgetting that there might be a young woman at her table who needs her to speak truth into her life and show it by her actions. She's forgetting that we will continue learning more of Christ through God's Word until the day we die. She's forgetting that she's a vital part of the covenant community. She's forgetting that she's not just in covenant with God but in a covenant relationship with God's people as well.[2]

Our relationships are to be ruled by God's Word. We are to exalt Christ in them. We are to love one another because God first loved us. We are to attend to each other's needs. We are to always point each other to the truth. We are to invest in each other's lives so that we can help each other run the Christian race with endurance. We are to give each other the opportunity to share our hearts freely and openly. We are not to neglect meeting together for corporate worship. We are to sing gospel truth to each other. We are to help each other when times are tough. We are to invite others to do life with us by asking them to pray for us and encourage us. We are to be peacemakers when conflict arises. And we are to strengthen each other with the truth of the gospel each and every day.

---

2. For more on this topic, see Sarah Ivill, *The Covenantal Life: Appreciating the Beauty of Theology and Community* (Grand Rapids: Reformation Heritage Books, 2018).

We Are Accountable to the Word of God

Finally, Genesis 1:27–28 reveals that we are in submission to the ultimate authority, the Word of God. God was King of the garden kingdom. His rules were to be obeyed, or there would be consequences. That means we are not free to be or do anything we want to be or do, contrary to what the world tells us. We are either walking in obedience to God or walking in disobedience to Him. We are to place ourselves in a posture of humility, laying our very lives on the altar for the Lord to do with as He pleases (again, see Rom. 12:1–2). But instead, as fallen creatures, we want to control our own lives, submitting to ourselves. This is why Paul labors in Ephesians 5:18–6:9 to speak about Spirit-filled submission. One of the ways by which we obey Paul's exhortation to "be filled with the Spirit" is by "submitting to one another in the fear of God" (Eph. 5:18, 21). He goes on to teach that wives are to submit to their husbands, children to their parents, and slaves to their masters. The key in each one of these situations is that submission is to take place as though one were submitting to the Lord (5:22; 6:1, 5–7). As those who have been saved by grace alone and given numerous spiritual blessings in Christ, we are to submit to God and to one another in fear and reverence of our Creator and Redeemer.

Psalm 19 gives us a beautiful description of God's Word. It is perfect. There is no other book on your bookshelf that is perfect. But God's Word is. The next time you need help, reach for God's Word. It also has the power to convert souls. I have known of men and women who were converted simply by reading Scripture. God's Word is sure and filled with wisdom. Before seeking a counselor, let us seek Scripture. It is righteous and has the power to make one's heart rejoice. It is pure. It enlightens one's eyes. It endures forever. It is true. It is to be desired more than the treasures of this world. It serves to both warn us of danger and encourage us toward faithfulness. It's a Word you don't want to be without; indeed, a Word you cannot be without. It is your very life. Moses told Israel, "Set your hearts on all the words which I testify among you today, which you shall command your children to be careful to observe—all the words of this law. For it is not a futile thing for you, because it is your life, and by this word you shall prolong your days in the land which you cross over the Jordan to possess" (Deut. 32:46–47).

Forgetting Who We Are Is Costly

Something tragic happens in Genesis 3. Eve forgets who she is (an image bearer of God who is to reflect His knowledge, righteousness, and holiness). And she forgets what she is supposed to do (worship, work, live out her design as woman alongside her husband, and obey the words of God). This has disastrous results.

> Now the serpent was more cunning than any beast of the field which the LORD God had made. And he said to the woman, "Has God indeed said, 'You shall not eat of every tree of the garden'?"
>
> And the woman said to the serpent, "We may eat the fruit of the trees of the garden; but of the fruit of the tree which is in the midst of the garden, God

has said, 'You shall not eat it, nor shall you touch it, lest you die.'"

Then the serpent said to the woman, "You will not surely die. For God knows that in the day you eat of it your eyes will be opened, and you will be like God, knowing good and evil." (Gen. 3:1–5)

Satan offers Eve what she already has—Eve is already like God! She has been created in His own image. But Eve has an impure thirst that leads to an imperfect world. She doesn't just want to be like God; she wants to be god in her own life. And on that tragic day in the garden when Eve believed Satan's lie, she rebelled against God's Word, and all humankind fell with Adam and Eve. The perfection and delight of the garden were marred by the putrid deceitfulness of sin.

According to 1 John 3:4, "sin is lawlessness." One Reformed catechism defines it this way: "Sin is rejecting or ignoring God in the world he created, rebelling against him by living without reference to him, not being or doing what he requires in his law—resulting in our death and the disintegration of all creation."[3] And because we reject and rebel against our Creator, resulting in spiritual death, we become idolaters. Idolatry occurs any time we exchange the truth about God for a lie and worship and serve the created instead of the Creator (Rom. 1:25). Or, as this catechism puts it, "Idolatry is trusting in created things rather than the Creator for our hope and happiness, significance and security."[4]

---

3. The New City Catechism, A. 16.
4. New City Catechism, A. 17.

Because our hearts are broken from the fall, we trust in broken cisterns instead of in our blessed Redeemer. We look to our health for our hope. We look to our hobbies for our happiness. We look to the stars on our children's report cards for our significance. And we look to our savings for security.

Thankfully, the tragedy of the fall is not the end of the story. Genesis 3:15 (the gospel in seed form) is close at hand, and we are going to take a long glimpse at the gospel in part 2 of this book, but for now I want us to focus on the effects of the fall on our thirst. In the next chapter we will look at how an impure thirst leads to disorder, discontentment, and death.

Can you relate to our family's Saturday? Have you ever wanted to surprise someone with something but couldn't get them away from what they thought was ample pleasure? The Lord has a treasure house of merciful riches for us, and yet we're often content to sit amidst broken cisterns. These can never satisfy our thirst because they're broken. Our thirst must always and only be satisfied in Christ.

Thinking It Through

1. Describe a time when you have tried to surprise someone with something, only to have them content to go
   on doing what they were doing, or when someone
   tried to surprise you with something and you were
   resistant to giving up your current activity.

2. If someone were to look at the way you devote your
   time, talents, and treasure, what would they say you
   worship?

3. In what ways did you work for the glory of God this
   week, and in what ways did you work for your own
   glory? You may want to ask a friend, your husband, or
   one of your children what they saw you working for
   this week.

4. Why do we tend toward isolationism and individualism instead of toward interdependence in the church?

5. How does your life reflect interdependence with your
   church family?

6. In what ways does your life reflect God's Word as your absolute authority?

7. How are you seeking to teach those under your leadership that God's Word is our final authority on all matters?

8. Spend time in prayer this week, asking the Lord to give you a desire for His glorious riches and to take away your affection for broken cisterns. Consider keeping a journal of your written prayers, along with other notes or answers to questions, as you study this book. Repent of worshiping, working for, and witnessing about that which is not for His glory. Then pray that you will worship, work, and witness for Him alone.

9. Seek to memorize Deuteronomy 32:46–47 this week. You may want to consider writing it out once a day to help you, or speaking it out loud three times a day.

Chapter 2

Disorder, Discontentment, and Death

Perhaps one of the issues I deal with the most often in discipling my children's hearts is discontentment. It's one of those sins that doesn't usually put us on our knees, like sexual promiscuity, alcoholism, or a foul mouth, but it becomes a constant irritant in the life of the home that, when left alone, gets very big and very ugly. It can start with that whiny summertime "I'm bored." Or "Why can't I have it?" Or "I want it now." I have noticed it in my own life as well. When I seem on edge with others, which is often those closest to me, like my children or husband, and I do a heart check, I often find a heart of discontentment. In other words, life isn't going my way at the moment, and I don't like it! I want something to be different than it is. And I am having a hard time accepting that it isn't.

I'm sure you can relate, but I wonder if we too often rationalize away discontentment in our lives as acceptable. Don't be fooled. Discontentment is destructive. It's inconsistent with the new heart we've been given in Christ. It's sin. It cares nothing for others but is completely self-focused. It's closefisted instead

of openhanded to God's purposes and plans. It's not
neighborly. It distorts truth. It envies. It's never timely.
And it torments the soul. In contrast, contentment finds
its home in Christ and cares for others. It's openhanded
to God's ways. It's neighborly. It believes truth. It does
not covet. It's always on time. And it trains the soul to
trust in the Lord at all times. In this chapter we'll look at
discontentment, as well as two other fruits of the flesh,
disorder and death.

An Overview

Disorder

I don't imagine any of us has escaped this word in our
lifetime. Whether it's a clinical diagnosis for ourselves,
loved ones, neighbors, or friends, conditions such
as anxiety disorders, eating disorders, attention defi-
cit disorders, and obsessive-compulsive disorders are
a reflection of the fallen world in which we live. But it
doesn't just have to be a clinical diagnosis. Disorder is all
around us. Because of the fall we have disordered desires
that come from a heart disorder, and this leads to different kinds of disorders in relationships at home, work,
church, and within the broader community. We've taken
good things and distorted them so that they've become
disordered affections in our lives that we serve as gods.

Discontentment

This diagnosis doesn't carry the same negative connota-
tion as the word *disorder*, but it's just as deadly to one's
soul. After all, discontentment is what got Israel into trouble in the wilderness; in fact, it cost them their life. They

were grumbling about not having meat to eat, recalling the good old days of Egypt (which hadn't actually been good), and the Lord got so angry that He sent a plague to destroy the complainers (Numbers 11). Discontentment is a fruit of the impure thirst of the flesh. We want something that we can't have, or we want something that we don't have, or we don't want something that we do have (see James 4:1–6). Discontentment breeds distrust in our deliverer, Jesus Christ, as we wrongly conclude that He's withholding His best from us. For example, it's been my experience in ministering to women that far more women believe in God's sovereignty than in His goodness. The woman longing for a baby, but whose arms remain empty year after year, usually believes that God is sovereign over her circumstances, but she has a hard time trusting His goodness toward her in that particular circumstance. But God's goodness is not based on our getting what we want when we want it. It is based on His covenant love, which is always perfectly kind, faithful, and true.

Death

Sometimes physical death is the result of a disorder, or even discontentment, but certainly spiritual death is. Adam and Eve's disordered and discontented hearts in the garden led to both spiritual and physical death. Disordered and discontented hearts have the same result today. Consider Proverbs 9:13–18:

> A foolish woman is clamorous....
> For she sits at the door of her house...
> To call to those who pass by,...

"Stolen water is sweet,
And bread eaten in secret is pleasant."
But he does not know that the dead are there,
That her guests are in the depths of hell.

In this chapter I want us to take a closer look at these three fruits of the flesh: disorder, discontentment, and death.

Disordered Desires

In Genesis 11:1–9 we read about a failed attempt among a people who wanted to make a name for themselves. The entire earth had one language at the time, and as people migrated from the east they settled together on one piece of land. They decided to build a city and a tower with its top reaching to the heavens so that they could make a name for themselves and stick together as a community of people. When the Lord saw this city and tower, He confused their language and dispersed them through-out the earth in order to destroy their ability to continue building a city and name for themselves. He judged them because they had exchanged worship of their Creator for worship of what they themselves had created.

The Tower of Babel illustrates for us that the lust for power, position, possessions, and prestige leads to confusion and disorder. The people lusted for bricks instead of God's blessings, a city instead of a Savior, a name for themselves instead of glorifying the name above all names, and a community founded on a human founda-tion and words instead of a community founded on God and His Word. The result was confusion and disorder.

God will not compete for the glory due to His name alone. He says, "You shall have no other gods before Me" (Ex. 20:3).

Confusion and disorder are what happened to Kay (see the introduction), who, despite all the accolades of others, was filled with anxiety. The desire to work hard in life and do well isn't bad in and of itself, but when it becomes the chief end of your life you've usurped God's chief end for humankind—to glorify Him and to enjoy Him forever.[1] Confusion and disorder are also what happened to Sarah, who worshiped the scale instead of her Savior. It's not that eating healthily and engaging in exercise are bad. Food and exercise are good gifts from our heavenly Father. But when food and fitness usurp the throne in our hearts that God alone is to sit on, we have a worship disorder that manifests itself in an eating disorder.

Like those who built the Tower of Babel, we put one brick of success on top of another until we have made a name for ourselves. We think that we can reach up to heaven with moralism instead of looking to the Master who has come down to us. He "made Himself of no reputation, taking the form of a bondservant, and coming in the likeness of men. And being found in appearance as a man, He humbled Himself and became obedient to the point of death, even the death of the cross" (Phil. 2:7–8). We engage in culture-building activities that exalt our human foundation and words instead of upholding Christ's words and resting in Him alone. "All Scripture is

1. Westminster Shorter Catechism, A. 1.

given by inspiration of God, and is profitable for doctrine, for reproof, for correction, for instruction in righteousness, that the man of God may be complete, thoroughly equipped for every good work" (2 Tim. 3:16–17).

Our thirst for power, position, possessions, and prestige leads to the same thing it did at the Tower of Babel—every kind of disorder we can imagine. This is not how God is. "God is not the author of confusion but of peace" (1 Cor. 14:33). Christ has come to deliver us from "contentions, jealousies, outbursts of wrath, selfish ambitions, backbitings, whisperings, conceits, tumults" (2 Cor. 12:20)—all things that usually accompany confusion and disorder. Read that list again slowly and out loud. If we're honest, our daily lives are filled with confusion and disorder. All of us get angry. All of us experience jealousy at someone or something. And in a culture that has taught us to claw our way to the top by achievements, we know what selfish ambition is. The good news of the gospel is that Christ offers us peace in Himself. "Peace I leave with you, My peace I give to you; not as the world gives do I give to you. Let not your heart be troubled, neither let it be afraid" (John 14:27).

The Daily News of Discontentment

Not only does our impure thirst lead to disorder; it also leads to discontentment. In Exodus 16:1–3 we read an account that occurred in the life of Israel during their early years of wandering through the wilderness on their way to the promised land. The previous chapters of Exodus recounted God's miraculous deliverance of Israel from Egypt. The Song of Moses had celebrated the

Lord's glorious triumph, and the people had boasted in His grand power. Miriam, Moses's sister, led the women in singing and dancing unto the Lord for His great victory. But then they came to the wilderness. Israel grumbled against the Lord during these days, displaying great discontentment. Their appetite was for the food they remembered eating in Egypt instead of for their Father above. Their physical hunger blinded them to God's truth, and they became spiritually starved. In the Wilderness of Sin they thought it would have been better to have died in Egypt than to endure hunger in the wilderness. Their memory failed them, deceiving them to think they had eaten meat and bread until they were full. The truth was that they had been slaves in the land of Egypt. The first several chapters of Exodus recount for us the miseries they had endured there. Discontentment always blinds us to the truth. It deceives us into thinking that our best days were in the past and that if only we could have them back we'd be satisfied.

We see a similar pattern to the one we saw in Genesis. Genesis 1 and 2 were filled with the amazing truth of creation, followed by the tragedy of Eve's impure thirst in chapter 3. Similarly, Exodus 14 and 15 are filled with the amazing truth of God's deliverance of Israel from Egypt, followed by the tragedy of Israel's grumbling in the wilderness. The people thirsted for a return to the pots of meat and plenteous bread of Egypt instead of drinking in the reality of God's presence with them in the wilderness. Their physical hunger blinded them to their spiritual hunger and the opportunity they had to feast on the goodness of the Lord as He provided for them and protected them on their journey.

Before we shake our heads at Israel, we need to recognize that we do the same thing. Oftentimes on the heels of God's wondrous works in our lives and after time spent feasting on God's wonderful Word, we hunger and thirst for a return to the things in our life that most tempt us to find our satisfaction apart from Christ. Our physical hunger blinds us to our spiritual hunger and the opportunity we have to feast on the goodness of the Lord through His Word, prayer, the sacraments, and fellowship with other believers. But this is exactly the prescription we need for the disease of discontentment.

Paul had learned the lesson of contentment through these means of grace: "I have learned in whatever state I am, to be content: I know how to be abased, and I know how to abound. Everywhere and in all things I have learned both to be full and to be hungry, both to abound and to suffer need. I can do all things through Christ who strengthens me" (Phil. 4:11–13). Christ strengthened Paul through the Word of God. You and I need to be in the Word if we're going to fight discontentment. He also strengthened Paul through prayer. Because Paul was a man of prayer, he exhorts believers to pray at all times, with all prayer and supplication in the Spirit, with all perseverance, and for all the saints (Eph. 6:18). Prayer realigns us to be content with what Christ has given to us. Christ also strengthened Paul through the sacraments and fellowship with other believers. As Paul interacted with those in the early church and joined them for worship on the Lord's Day, he was strengthened to fight discontentment and be content in Christ.

We see another example of impure thirst leading to discontentment in 1 Samuel 8:4–9. The elders of Israel gathered together and approached Samuel, demanding a king to judge them like all the nations around them. Such a request was very displeasing to Samuel, so he prayed to the Lord. The Lord heard Samuel and answered him, telling Samuel to give Israel what they wanted. It wasn't Samuel they were rejecting, but the Lord as king. Just as they had forsaken the Lord since the days after He had delivered them from Egypt, so they were forsaking God through His representative, Samuel. The Lord told Samuel that he was to grant their request with a warning to go along with it. The kind of king the people were demanding would be difficult to endure. Israel thirsted for a king like the other nations and, despite Samuel's solemn warnings, demanded the king of their own choosing, rejecting the Lord. Such thirst turned out to be disastrous and destructive, leaving Israel with empty hands.

Oftentimes we demand something from the Lord that we want because we perceive that "everyone else" has it. Has your child ever come home and asked you for something you had to say no to? And then they said, "Mom, everybody else has one." And you reply, "Everyone?" Of course everyone else doesn't have one, but they've been deceived into believing that their delight lies in that demand being met, and they are discontented until they get whatever it is. We do the same thing. It's a grown-up version, but just as sinful. Perhaps we want the

bigger house, bigger car, or bigger vacation that many
of our peers have. Maybe we want a godly husband, but
another year of singleness goes by. Or maybe we want a
house full of children, and the road of infertility seems
too hard. Perhaps we want an easier life with less work.
Maybe we are tired of chronic pain.

In each case the temptation is to demand our desires
from the Lord. Such thirst often turns out to be disastrous and destructive, leaving us with empty hands,
tickled ears, and shattered hearts. Paul says, "Now godliness with contentment is great gain. For we brought
nothing into this world, and it is certain we can carry
nothing out" (1 Tim. 6:6–7). Christ wants more for us
than the empty materialism of this world. He wants to fill
our hands with His nail-pierced ones, to fill our ears with
His Word, and to overwhelm our hearts with His love so
that we might love Him, enjoy Him, trust Him, and obey
Him (a topic we will return to in part 3 of this book).

The Devastation of Death

Not only does impure thirst lead to disorder and discontentment; it also leads to death. The Bible tells us
that "the wages of sin is death" (Rom. 6:23). We defined
sin in the last chapter as lawlessness (1 John 3:4). It may
also be described as "rejecting or ignoring God in the
world he created, rebelling against him by living without
reference to him, not being or doing what he requires
in his law—resulting in our death and the disintegration of all creation."[2] Such sin cannot go unpunished

---

2. New City Catechism, A. 16.

because "every sin is against the sovereignty, holiness, and goodness of God, and against his righteous law, and God is righteously angry with our sins and will punish them in his just judgment both in this life, and in the life to come."[3]

King David, a man after God's own heart, thirsted for a woman who was not his own and got her pregnant, only to watch their child die, arrange to have her husband murdered in battle, and finally marry her (2 Samuel 11–12). His thirst was disastrous for his household, Bathsheba, and his kingdom. In the aftermath of the event David cried,

> Have mercy upon me, O God,
> According to Your lovingkindness;
> According to the multitude of Your tender
>   mercies,
> Blot out my transgressions.
> Wash me thoroughly from my iniquity,
> And cleanse me from my sin.
>
> For I acknowledge my transgressions,
> And my sin is always before me.
> Against You, You only, have I sinned,
> And done this evil in Your sight. (Ps. 51:1–4)

Before we can shake our heads at David, we are reminded of our own lusts of the flesh that lead to the same disastrous and deadly results for our marriages and families. It may or may not be adultery or murder,

---

3. New City Catechism, A. 18.

but when we thirst for romance from a book instead of from our husband, or when we exchange true love in a monogamous relationship for the lust of a one-night stand, or when we murder our neighbor in our heart with our anger, or when we gossip about a woman at work, we plunge headlong into disaster.

This is what happened to Amy (see the introduction), who escaped into sexual sin instead of engaging in healthy relationships with others. Paul said to the Corinthians, "Flee sexual immorality…. Your body is the temple of the Holy Spirit who is in you, whom you have from God…. You were bought at a price; therefore glorify God in your body and in your spirit, which are God's" (1 Cor. 6:18–20). Similarly, he pleaded for purity among the Thessalonians: "For this is the will of God, your sanctification: that you should abstain from sexual immorality; that each of you should know how to possess his own vessel in sanctification and honor…. For God did not call us to uncleanness, but in holiness" (1 Thess. 4:3–4, 7).

I have used these verses with my children, teaching them from a young age a biblical view of sexuality and exhorting them toward purity. If we're not talking to our children about sex, the world will. We need to help them understand the gift of sex within marriage, as well as the consequences when we remove the gift from its proper context. Purity is not old-fashioned or obsolete. It is God's plan for His people, and He enables us to be pure, as He is pure.

The Bible's wisdom literature also testifies to the truth that impure thirst leads to death. In Proverbs 7:10–23 we read of a wayward wife whose husband was away on a trip. While he was gone she pursued another man in order to have an affair with him. Proverbs tells us that many have followed the seductive voice of this woman and stepped into the chambers of death because of it. At times we are the women who use seductive speech and smooth talk to compel others to like us or follow us. At other times we are the women who are seduced by such speech and march to the death of a dream, relationship, or career. Regardless, the staircase leads to the same spiritual death.

The prophets testify to the same truth that impure thirst leads to death. The Lord declared through Jeremiah,

> "For My people have committed two evils:
> They have forsaken Me, the fountain of
>   living waters,
> And hewn themselves cisterns—broken
>   cisterns that can hold no water."
> (Jer. 2:13)

The human heart is a hewer of cisterns that continually drain water. When we run out of water in our bodies, we die! The same is true of us spiritually. We are dead in our trespasses and sins (Eph. 2:1), unable to resuscitate ourselves. Jeremiah says that our hearts are deceitful above all things and desperately sick (Jer. 17:9–10). It is only the Lord who can understand our hearts because He searches them and tests our minds. He came to make the sick heart well. He came to give us a new heart (a topic we'll talk more about in part 2 of this book). No wonder

Paul prayed for the Ephesian church "that the God of
our Lord Jesus Christ, the Father of glory, may give to
you the spirit of wisdom and revelation in the knowledge of Him, the eyes of your understanding [hearts,
ESV] being enlightened; that you may know what is the
hope of His calling, what are the riches of the glory of
His inheritance in the saints, and what is the exceeding
greatness of His power toward us who believe" (Eph.
1:17–19). Jesus came to set us free from spiritual death,
as well as from the sting of physical death. Everyone who
puts their faith in Him as Lord and Savior will live forever with Him in the new heaven and the new earth.
Though we will still die (unless we're alive at Christ's second coming), death for the believer is the end of a life
of suffering and sin and the glorious beginning of being
with Jesus forever.

Perhaps disorder, discontentment, or death of some
kind is lurking beneath the surface of your heart. Or
maybe you are aware that it's there and are striving to
put it to death. Regardless, this chapter has continued
to reveal our need for the living water that Christ offers
us (a topic we'll turn to in part 2 of this book). But for
now, since we've traced this theme of impure thirst
through the Old Testament and have seen that it leads
to an imperfect world filled with disorder, discontentment, and death, let's take a closer look at what the New

Testament has to say about our impure thirsts. In the next chapter we will learn how our impure thirst leads to impure passions and incorrect doctrine.

Thinking It Through

1. Briefly describe a recent time when you found yourself discontented. How did you handle it?

2. When you think about disorder, discontentment, and death as they work themselves out in your own life, what is going on in your heart at those moments? In other words, what tempts you to believe that worldly ways are better than God's ways?

3. How can you relate to those at the Tower of Babel who were building a name for themselves? What does the Tower of Babel teach you about God's priorities?

4. In what ways do you battle the sin of discontentment?

5. When has your memory failed you, deceiving you into thinking things were better in the past than they really were?

6. What passages of Scripture referred to in this chapter pertaining to discontentment were most helpful for you?

7. In what ways can you relate to David's sin and confession?

8. Spend time in prayer, asking the Lord to deliver you from any discontentment, disorder, or destructive habits you've been convicted of while studying this chapter.

9. Seek to memorize 2 Timothy 3:16–17 this week.

Chapter 3

Impure Passions and Incorrect Doctrine

She was raised in a Christian home, attended church each Sunday, was baptized, and partook regularly of the Lord's Supper. She shared her faith boldly and was active and involved in the youth group. But she chose a rebellious lifestyle. And because she did, she had to change her doctrine. Denying Christ as Lord and Savior of her life and declaring that she served another god, she turned her back on the Christian doctrines she'd known for so long and embraced a doctrine filled with deceit.

I have heard a similar version of this story repeatedly during the many years I've served in women's ministry. A son or daughter, sibling or extended relative, friend or neighbor raised in the faith, baptized in the church, and on fire for a time for the Lord, turns their back on the Lord to live a different lifestyle. And because they do, they have to change their doctrine. In this chapter we will look closely at the impure passions of our hearts, where they come from, and how they lead us to embrace incorrect doctrine.

The Impure Passions of Our Hearts

When Adam and Eve fell into sin (and all humankind with them), something terrible happened to our hearts. They became "deceitful above all things, and desperately wicked" (Jer. 17:9). Our hearts became a brewery of impure passions. These passions rage in our hearts so strongly that Scripture says we're in a battle between the flesh and the Spirit (Rom. 7:21–23; Gal. 5:17; Eph. 6:10–20). Jesus teaches us that "those things which proceed out of the mouth come from the heart, and they defile a man. For out of the heart proceed evil thoughts, murders, adulteries, fornications, thefts, false witness, blasphemies" (Matt. 15:18–19). Jesus exposes our hearts for the cesspools of sin they are. Our hearts are factories of evil. When was the last time you had an evil thought? When was the last time you murdered someone with your words or looks? When was the last time you engaged in sexual sin? When was the last time you stole something from someone? When was the last time you misrepresented someone with your words? It's likely that if you're honest, one or more of these issues was brewing in your heart today. Of course, we are to turn away from such sin to our Savior, something we will look at in greater detail in parts 2 and 3 of this book. But for now I want you to recognize that our hearts produce pools of passions that aren't pure.

Paul's list of fleshly fruits in Galatians is even more extensive than the one in Matthew. "Now the works of the flesh are evident, which are: adultery, fornication, uncleanness, lewdness, idolatry, sorcery, hatred, contentions, jealousies, outbursts of wrath, selfish ambitions, dissensions, heresies, envy, murders, drunkenness, rev-elries, and the like" (Gal. 5:19–21). Not one person can honestly look at this list and say they aren't battling against one or another or several of these vices. Take "outbursts of wrath," for example. When was the last time you felt anger rise from your feet to your face? Did your husband irritate you? Did your children disrupt your comfort? Did someone in the ministry take credit for something you did, or an idea you had? And if so, did you raise your voice at them? Or what about "selfish ambitions"? Often-times we don't know we have selfish ambitions until we don't get the promotion or praise we wanted. Our reac-tion in the face of failure reveals the ambitions of our hearts. Too many times we're out to make a name for ourselves instead of making God's name great.

James brings this discussion on impure passions a bit closer to home. "Where do wars and fights come from among you? Do they not come from your desires for pleasure that war in your members? You lust and do not have. You murder and covet and cannot obtain. You fight and war.... Adulterers and adulteresses! Do you not know that friendship with the world is enmity with God?" (James 4:1–2, 4). Our impure passions arise from the flesh within us, are applauded by the world around us, and are an armory for the devil and his minions, who are constantly prowling around us. While these are things we want to hide from each other, James assumes there are wars and fights among us. He knows that we lust and covet. He knows we fight and war. But he breaks into our silence and says "Stop!" If we choose impure passions, we choose to have an affair with the world, forsaking our covenant relationship with the Lord God. When we find ourselves in these moments, let us cry out to God to enable us to flee the flesh, stand firm against Satan, and withstand the world. "God resists the proud, but gives grace to the humble" (James 4:6)—to those who humble themselves and cry for help.

Finding Our Impure Passions

In many cases we know what trips us up and sends us into a downward spiral on the path of rebellion. But remember, our hearts are deceitful, and so many times we are caught off guard or are blinded to our impure passions. This is where asking good questions can be really helpful. Take some time this week to honestly ponder the health of your heart by asking yourself the following:

* When do I feel most satisfied with myself? My family? My church?

* What must I have in order to be happy?

* What do I have to do each day in order to feel good about myself?

* To what or whom do I give the majority of my time and devotion?

* In what ways do I take credit that should go to God alone?

* What drives my work ethic?

* Do I rest and worship on Sundays, and if not, why not?

* How do I relate to those who lead me, and how do I relate to those who follow me?

* When I get angry, what tends to have been threatened at that moment—my comfort, control, character, or convenience?

* What forms of sexual immorality am I most prone to engage in?

* How am I tempted to use my time, talents, and treasure for my desires instead of for the Lord and His church?

* In what ways am I tempted to speak badly of my neighbor, and why?

* In what circumstances does envy most often seize me? What do I want that the other person has, and why do I want it?

This exercise has proved helpful at different times in my life. In my early twenties I answered the question "What do I have to do each day in order to feel good about myself" with the answer "I have to exercise and eat healthily." This helped me recognize an impure passion of my heart. I had become addicted to thinness and fitness.[1] This is where the heart can be so deceitful. Fitness isn't bad in and of itself. There is great benefit to it. But when it becomes something we must have in order to feel good about ourselves, we have elevated fitness to a

---

1. For the fuller story, see my book *Never Enough: Confronting Lies about Appearance and Achievement with Gospel Hope* (Grand Rapids: Reformation Heritage Books, 2019).

place on the throne of our hearts that Christ alone must occupy. In other words, if at any time we can't say "Christ is enough for me" and really mean it, then we know it's time to evaluate. Oftentimes I have had to confess that I want Christ plus marriage, or children, or another ministry opportunity, or comfort or convenience, or the like. It's a great mercy, even if it's grievous and grueling to work through, when the Lord reveals to us where our passions have strayed. May we be quick to confess and run toward repentance so that we might find sweet fellowship with our Father again.

Feeding Our Impure Passions

When Cain should have continued working the ground for the Lord's glory and offering sacrifices to Him with a pure and undefiled heart, he instead resented the Lord's kind regard of his brother, Abel, and his sacrifice. His impure passions of envy, resentment, and anger in his heart led to the murder of his brother by his own hands (Gen. 4:1–8).

When Lot's wife should have obeyed the Lord's word through the angel to not look back at the city that was being destroyed by fire because of its sinfulness, she instead looked back at the sinful cities of Sodom and Gomorrah. Her impure passion of putting her desires ahead of the Lord's and not heeding His warning cost her life (Gen. 19:17, 26).

When Samson should have honored the Lord, as well as his mother and father, by taking a wife from his own people instead of the Philistines, he instead sinfully demanded the fulfillment of his impure passions. First he saw a woman and wanted her. Then he demanded her: "Get her for me, for she pleases me well" (Judg. 14:3). The impure passion of his eyes led to a sinful marriage.

When King David should have been at war instead of at home, sin struck. From the rooftop of his house he saw the beautiful Bathsheba bathing. Instead of turning away from the impure passion of his heart, he acted on it. He asked others who this woman was and then sent for her. Once she was in his presence, he fed his impure passion of lust and committed adultery (2 Sam. 11:1–5). As the story unfolds, we learn that his adultery led to following through on another impure passion by committing murder. In trying to cover up one sin he committed another (11:6–27).

When King Solomon should have clung to the Lord's command to not marry women who followed other gods because they would turn Solomon's heart away from following the true God, he instead clung to his many foreign wives. As the story unfolds, we learn that Solomon actually enabled each of his foreign wives to worship their gods by building high places of worship for them (1 Kings 11:1–8). His impure passion of lust led him to forsake his first love of the Lord, and in the end it led to the downfall of the kingdom (11:9–40).

When Ananias and Sapphira should have given all the money they received from the sale of their land as they had committed to do, they instead conceived evil in their hearts and lied to both men and God, pretending to give the full amount when they really withheld some for themselves. Their impure passion of greed cost them their lives (Acts 5:1–11).

When Euodia and Syntyche, two women in the Philippian church, should have been of the same mind in the Lord, they instead disagreed about a matter and brought disunity within the church. Paul had to exhort these women, who had labored for the gospel alongside him, to dwell in unity, and he had to exhort the entire church to help them do so (Phil. 4:2–3).

In each one of these situations sin was conceived in the heart by the interworking of three things: the lust of the flesh, the lust of the eyes, and the pride of life. The apostle John says, "Do not love the world or the things in the world. If anyone loves the world, the love of the Father is not in him. For all that is in the world—the lust of the flesh, the lust of the eyes, and the pride of life—is not of the Father but is of the world. And the world is passing away, and the lust of it; but he who does the will of God abides forever" (1 John 2:15–17).

There are several things we can learn from these verses. First, our sinful nature is to love the world. This means that our flesh will want what this world has to offer. To forget that is very costly. If you think you can walk into a certain setting, whether it's the beach or the bar, the mall or the magazine aisle, the academy or the arcade, and not be tempted, you are already in trouble. You need to know as you go about life that your flesh loves the things of this world. Second, believers have been given the power to not love the world. The Holy Spirit enables us to truly, though not yet perfectly, love the Father. This is because the love of the Father is in us, and He has changed us and is changing us, enabling us to love Him and not the world. Third, the lust of the flesh and the eyes and the pride of life all work in tandem to tempt us. When our own flesh, which is already filled with impure passions, sees something we want with our eyes, and we believe the lie that we deserve it and have earned it, we will choose to walk the way of the world instead of the way of the Word every time.

Finally, the prescription for loving the Father instead of the world is to do the will of God. What does this mean? Paul sheds great light on this in his letter to the Thessalonians: "For this is the will of God, your sanctification: that you should abstain from sexual immorality; that each of you should know how to possess his own vessel in sanctification and honor, not in passion of lust" (1 Thess. 4:3–5). We must put to death the passions of impurity by knowing how to possess our person in purity. We cannot do this apart from Christ. But in Him we are new creatures and have resurrection power within us to fight against the flesh with the full armor of God, which includes knowing who we are in Christ, recognizing the power of the Holy Spirit, and standing firm on the truth of Scripture (Eph. 6:10–20). Doing these things, while at the same time praying in perseverance, will put up resistance when the world wants to swallow us whole, our flesh wants to stop fighting, and the devil dangles desires and deceit before us. Let our cry be "Help us, Lord! We cannot win this battle unless You fight for us and enable us to stand strong!"

Impure Passions Feed Incorrect Doctrine

Paul, in speaking to Timothy about the importance of preaching God's Word in season and out of season, informs him that "the time will come when [perilous men] will not endure sound doctrine, but according to their own desires, because they have itching ears, they will heap up for themselves teachers; and they will turn their ears away from the truth, and be turned aside to fables" (2 Tim. 4:3–4). These are the kind of men "who creep into households and make captives of gullible women loaded down with sins, led away by various lusts, always learning and never able to come to the knowledge of the truth" (2 Tim. 3:6–7). Notice that we are susceptible to doctrinal deceit when we are loaded down with sin, when lust leads us astray, and when accepting lies leads to an endless lust for knowledge that never satisfies because it is devoid of truth.

We love to surround ourselves with those who will feed our impure passions instead of starve them. So we surround ourselves with people who convince us that our sin is okay, tell us to indulge in it, applaud us in the midst of it, and teach us that it is fine and right to continue in it. I have never had anyone tell me that they left a church because the teaching was too good or too sound. Instead, they leave because they are not hearing what they want to hear. The leaders are no longer feeding their impure passions; instead, they are trying to starve those passions with sound doctrine. So we move on to another place, or another mentor, or another friendship where truth is watered down a little bit more, and a little bit more, until we find a place where we feel we can be who we are, and do what we want to do, without anyone challenging our impure thirsts.

When I was in seminary one of my assignments for a theology class was to go to a place of worship that was different from my own. One week I went to the Cathedral of Hope, which claims to be the largest liberal "Christian" church reaching out primarily to the homosexual and transgender community. After the service I perused their bookstore. Not surprisingly, each resource I looked at fed the impure passions of the congregation with incorrect doctrine. For example, one book claimed that David and Jonathan's relationship was a gay one and used this story of these two men to reinforce their claim that the Bible approves of the gay lifestyle. I left that day deeply distressed at the deceptive doctrine being delivered from the pulpit, counseling center, and bookstore.

If we're going to meet the desires of our impure thirsts, we are going to have to change our doctrine from true to false. We can't feed our flesh while testifying to truth. Pure doctrine and impure passions are on a collision course. Correct doctrine drives pure passions. Incorrect doctrine drives impure ones. This means that one of the greatest prescriptions for impure passions is sound doctrine, which comes by a consistent and continual study of Scripture, and placing ourselves under the preaching of God's Word at a gospel-centered, Bible-believing church each Sunday. This is why Paul tells Timothy, "Preach the word! Be ready in season and out of season. Convince, rebuke, exhort, with all longsuffering and teaching" (2 Tim. 4:2). It's also why he tells Titus to have the older women in the church "speak the things which are proper for sound doctrine" (Titus 2:1) to the younger women. Sound doctrine leads to "reverent...behavior" and "teachers of good things" (v. 3). It's only when older women are grounded in sound doctrine that they can disciple younger women in truth that transforms their hearts and homes, minds and marriages (vv. 4–5). Instead of feeding our impure passions with incorrect doctrine, we need to help each other fast from them and be grateful when a sister in Christ wants to help us do so. Such discipleship can be informal or formal, but the goal is the same—"that you may be filled with the knowledge of His will in all wisdom and spiritual understanding; that you may walk worthy of the Lord, fully pleasing Him, being fruitful in every good work and increasing in the knowledge of God; strengthened with all might, according to His glorious power, for all patience and longsuffering with joy; giving thanks to the Father who has qualified us to be partakers of the inheritance of the saints in the light" (Col. 1:9–12).

It's likely that the story in the introduction to this chapter is very familiar to you. Whether you can personally identify with the young woman who changed her doctrine to meet her impure thirsts or whether your heart was breaking as you read it because someone you love has chosen to embrace their impure passions and has fallen into incorrect doctrine because of it, it's a story we've all heard many times in the church today. Above all else, we need to return to sound doctrine that saturates our minds with truth and transforms the passions of our hearts to that which is pure. We will talk more about this in the next two sections of this book, but before we do that let's take one last look at our impure thirsts in the next chapter. Our impure thirsts don't lead only to disorder, discontentment, death, impure passions, and incorrect doctrine; they also lead to enslavement and irreversible consequences.

Thinking It Through

1. Think of someone you know whose story is similar to the one in the introduction to this chapter. Spend time in prayer for him or her, asking the Lord to bring them "to their senses" and to enable them to "escape the snare of the devil, having been taken captive by him to do his will" (2 Tim. 2:26).

2. What did you learn from Scripture about the impure passions of our hearts? Against which ones do you battle the most?

3. Spend time this week going through the questions under "Finding Our Impure Passions." What did you learn?

4. Consider using the questions under "Finding Our Impure Passions" with those under your leadership, whether it's one of your own children, someone you disciple, or women in a small group you lead. Then commit to pray for them and hold them accountable.

5. According to Scripture, how do we feed our impure passions? Give an example of how you have seen this pattern in your own life.

6. How do impure passions feed incorrect doctrine, or vice versa? Give an example of how you have seen this work in your own life, or in the life of someone you know.

7. Spend time in daily prayer this week for your church, asking the Lord to help the pastors, elders, deacons, and other leaders to faithfully proclaim the Word of God in season and out of season. Consider writing at least one of them a note of encouragement, letting them know you are praying for them.

8. If you're an older woman, what discipleship opportunities do you have in which you can teach a younger woman sound doctrine and how to apply it to all of life? Consider being active and involved in doing this, either informally or formally. If you're a younger woman, consider asking an older woman in your church to teach you sound doctrine.

9. Seek to memorize 2 Timothy 2:24–26 this week.

Chapter 4

Enslavement and Infinite Consequences

Over the twenty-plus years I have been involved in women's ministry, I have had the privilege of praying for several people, many of whom were either enslaved by the things of this world and facing huge consequences or were impacted by someone who was. I have prayed for teens and women battling eating disorders. I have prayed for marriages threatened by adultery. I have prayed for teenagers battling deep depression. And I have prayed for men or women living a homosexual lifestyle. Regardless of the situation and the consequences, each situation demonstrates that the person is enslaved to a different master than Christ. In this chapter we will take a closer look at how we become enslaved to sin and the infinite consequences we face if we refuse to repent and turn to Christ.

Sin's Desire Is for You

Cain's countenance fell because his competitive spirit couldn't bear that the Lord respected Abel's offering instead of his. Competition always gets us into trouble; we need contentment in Christ. The Lord said to him,

"If you do well, will you not be accepted? And if you do not do well, sin lies at the door. And its desire is for you, but you should rule over it" (Gen. 4:7). Unfortunately, Cain didn't rule over his sin. Sin ruled over him, and the anger that arose in his heart led to the deliberate murder of his brother, Abel. We need to have the image of sin crouching at the door of our hearts, desiring to rule over us before we can, with the enablement of the Holy Spirit, rule over it instead. For example, if you know that you are prone to anger with your children at five o'clock in the afternoon after a long day at home with them, you need to remember that sin is crouching at the door of your heart. In this way, you will be prepared to fight the temptation and say no to anger and yes to righteousness in your home. Or, if you know you'll be tempted to binge on the ice cream in your freezer, you need to remember that sin is crouching at the door of your heart. Maybe you should flee the freezer, not bring the ice cream home in the first place, or have a friend hold you accountable.

Solomon fell from purity because sin was crouching at the door of his heart in the form of lust. He "loved many foreign women" from nations with which the Lord had forbidden intermarriage. "He had seven hundred wives, princesses, and three hundred concubines; and his wives turned away his heart.... His heart was not loyal to the LORD his God.... Solomon did evil in the sight of the LORD" (1 Kings 11:1, 3–4, 6). Because of his sin the Lord tore the kingdom away from Solomon's son (11:12–13). Wise King Solomon wasn't so wise in the face of sin.

We should learn several lessons from these devastating stories. First, sin is powerful. King Solomon had a good father, a tremendous ministry career, and so much wisdom that people from all over the world came to hear him speak. But because he didn't rule over the sin crouching at the door of his heart, welcoming it instead, he plunged headlong into sin, reaping the consequences for it. Second, sin is never personal. It always affects other people. Solomon's sin had devastating effects for the entire kingdom. The nation split into the northern kingdom of Israel and the southern kingdom of Judah, and both kingdoms had an entire line of (mostly) ungodly kings. Third, it is possible to rule over sin. The Lord told Cain that if he did well, meaning that if he obeyed the Lord and walked in His ways, then he would rule over the sin that desired to rule him. Let us never think that we're beyond falling headlong into a certain sin. Let us never forget that sin always has consequences, both for others and for us. And let us never forget that we have a choice to make in those moments when sin is crouching at the door of our hearts. By God's grace, we can choose to say no to sin's rule and yes to the Spirit's rule in our lives.

Slaves of Sin or Slaves of Righteousness?

Paul, in his letter to the Galatians, was concerned for the believers because, after having known God, they were turning again to bondage. In the context, they were forgetting the true gospel and turning to the observation of the ceremonial law. Paul says, "Stand fast therefore in the liberty by which Christ has made us free, and do not be entangled again with a yoke of bondage" (Gal. 5:1). Isn't that so often the case in our lives? God has chosen us, and we have enjoyed the benefits of a covenant relationship with Him, yet we want to turn back to gods we served earlier in our lives. When we do this, we often become enslaved to them.

In Paul's letter to Titus he reminds him that they both were at one time "serving various lusts and pleasures" (Titus 3:3). But when the kindness and love of God appeared, He saved them through Jesus Christ. Therefore, those who have believed in God and received justification should maintain works that are good and profitable for humankind (see 3:4–8). Christ has come to set us free from enslavement to sin so that we can be slaves of righteousness for Him. To return to slavery is to turn our back on the only Savior we have.

In his letter to the Romans Paul addresses the issue that we were once slaves to sin: "For just as you presented your members as slaves of uncleanness…" (Rom. 6:19). This is what happens when we give ourselves over to certain sins in our lives. We are actually presenting ourselves as slaves to anger, beauty, drugs, entertainment, food, fitness, shopping, social media, and sexual immorality. Instead, Paul goes on in this verse, "present your members as slaves of righteousness for holiness."

Whatever Overcomes Us, to That We Are Enslaved
In Peter's second letter we are warned about enslavement, or bondage in some Bible translations. Peter is warning God's people about false prophets and teachers in chapter 2. He says about them,

> These are wells without water, clouds carried by
> a tempest, for whom is reserved the blackness of
> darkness forever.
>
> For when they speak great swelling words of
> emptiness, they allure through the lusts of the
> flesh, through lewdness, the ones who have actually
> escaped from those who live in error. While they
> promise them liberty, they themselves are slaves
> of corruption; for by whom a person is overcome,
> by him also he is brought into bondage. (2 Peter
> 2:17–19)

There are several things we should note here. First, we
need to be aware that people will try to allure us through
the lusts of the flesh. Promises will prove to be empty.
Liberties are prisons laid open in our pathway. If we take
the bait, we'll be in bondage because whatever overcomes a person, to that he is enslaved.

This is what happened to Carol, whom we met in
the introduction. What started out as a moderate use of
social media turned into an unhealthy dependence on
it. Social media allures through the lusts of the flesh. The
perfection, performance, and promotion we all crave
are promised in myriad ways. Ironically, social media is
also the place where we question our perfection, performance, and promotion the most. If we don't get as
many likes on social media as we want, or if people don't
comment on how beautiful we look or what a great job
we did, we're tempted to think those things define our
worth. Scripture tells us differently. Scripture says we're
defined by Christ's perfect obedience and His atoning
death. Not only has He lived for us; He has also died for

us. He has set us free from slavery to social media and the other lusts of this world.

The book of Proverbs also speaks of slavery to sin:

> A foolish woman…
> sits at the door of her house…
> To call to those who pass by….
> And as for him who lacks understanding,
>   she says to him,
> "Stolen water is sweet,
> And bread eaten in secret is pleasant."
> But he does not know that the dead are there,
> That her guests are in the depths of hell.
>   (9:13–18)

This man is at a feast! Ironic, isn't it? He has beverages all around him that boast of the ability to quench one's thirst! But he is overcome by folly, and it lands him in the grave. Notice what happened. He was on the straight path, but he lacked sense and was seduced into a feast in the grave. Impure thirst leads to enslavement. But the opposite is also true. Pure thirst leads to freedom (John 8:36), which we will look at in the next part of this book. But let's look at one final point. According to Scripture, impure thirst doesn't just lead to an imperfect world, disorder, discontentment, death, impure passions, incorrect doctrine, and enslavement but also leads to infinite consequences.

Passions That Pull

Paul's words to Timothy about younger widows in the church are jarring: "But refuse the younger widows; for when they have begun to grow wanton against Christ, they desire to marry, having condemnation because they have cast off their first faith. And besides they learn to be idle, wandering about from house to house, and not only idle but also gossips and busybodies, saying things which they ought not" (1 Tim. 5:11–13). Certainly you and I know young widows who are exemplary in the faith. But apparently Paul was aware of a large group of young widows whose passions had pulled them away from Christ. Such impure passions had led to condemnation since they'd rejected their former faith, which is the only faith that could have saved them. In light of this passage, we need to be very wary of passions that might pull us away from Christ, of abandoning the faith, of idleness, of gossip, and of being a busybody instead of being busy about the body of Christ for the glory of God.

And Such Were Some of You
In writing to the Corinthian church, Paul had his hands full. This congregation was not the poster child for peace and purity. At the end of his admonishment against brothers bringing lawsuits against brothers, Paul says, "Do you not know that the unrighteous will not inherit the kingdom of God? Do not be deceived. Neither fornicators, nor idolaters, nor adulterers, nor homosexuals, nor sodomites, nor thieves, nor covetous, nor drunkards, nor revilers, nor extortioners will inherit the kingdom of God" (1 Cor. 6:9–10). Look closely at this list. Enslavement to sin and its infinite, irreversible consequences are closely linked. Yet there is hope. Paul goes on to say, "And such were some of you. But you were

washed, but you were sanctified, but you were justified in
the name of the Lord Jesus and by the Spirit of our God"
(1 Cor. 6:11). The only way out of enslavement to sin and
its tragic, infinite consequences is through faith in Jesus
Christ. He is the truth, and it is the truth that sets us free
(John 8:32; 14:6).

The Cup of Judgment

Because God is perfectly holy, He cannot tolerate sin.
He sent His Son into this world to save His people, but
there is coming a day when His wrath will fall upon the
rebellious. Psalm 75:8 teaches,

> For in the hand of the LORD there is a cup,
> And the wine is red;
> It is fully mixed, and He pours it out;
> Surely its dregs shall all the wicked of the earth
> Drain and drink down.

The doctrine of eternal punishment is difficult to proclaim, yet if we don't we're only telling others half the
gospel. Christ has come to offer us eternal life instead of
eternal separation from fellowship with God. Apart from
God's grace, all humankind will remain dead in their
trespasses and sins (Eph. 2:1).

If we choose to thirst for the impure things of this
world and reject God, we will drink the cup of judgment
and be separated from His presence, peace, and protection forever. He gives warning after warning in His
Word of such consequences. Thankfully, He is slow to
judgment, longing for us to come to repentance (2 Peter
3:9). Today is the day of salvation (2 Cor. 6:2). So I need

to ask you, dear reader, do you know Christ's love for you, and do you love Christ? Do you know the degree to which Christ has served you, and do you serve Him as Lord and Savior? Do you trust Him with your life? Do you obey His commands?

In the Gospels we learn that Jesus drank the cup of judgment so that you and I don't have to. This wasn't easy; before He died on the cross He had prayed in the garden of Gethsemane, "O My Father, if it is possible, let this cup pass from Me; nevertheless, not as I will, but as You will" (Matt. 26:39). Furthermore, Christ lived a life of perfect thirst in our place. He thirsted only for that which was righteous, fulfilling the law that you and I could never have fulfilled. What you are thirsting for matters, not just for now but for all eternity. If we thirst for the temporal we will die, but if we thirst for the eternal we will spend an eternity with Jesus Christ.

I want to remind you as we conclude part 1 of this book of Carol, Sarah, Gina, Amy, Lisa, Kay, and Tammy. Maybe you can relate to the emptiness of social media, health and beauty, shopping, sexual sin, busyness, achievement, or elevating motherhood to fulfill a need it was never meant to fulfill. If you have tried (as I have) to find fulfillment from any of these things, you know what it's like to be enslaved. I hope and pray that the truths in this book will help you find hope in the truth that Jesus has come to set you free from your impure thirsts so that you can thirst for the Fountain of living water, the topic we will address in the next part of this book.

Our hearts should be filled with compassion for those enslaved to sin and those facing its eternal consequences. As believers, we should fervently pray for the Lord to deliver them from such slavery so that they can present themselves as slaves of righteousness for holy living. Except for the grace of God, you and I could easily be entangled in the same addiction and facing the same consequences. As we close this chapter and move into the next part of this book, Jude's words are appropriate:

> Now to Him who is able to keep you from
>   stumbling,
> And to present you faultless
> Before the presence of His glory with
>   exceeding joy,
> To God our Savior,
> Who alone is wise,
> Be glory and majesty,
> Dominion and power,
> Both now and forever.
> Amen. (Jude 24–25)

Thinking It Through

1. How is the imagery of sin crouching at the door of your heart helpful in battling certain sins you presently face?

2. In what ways has social media ensnared you or someone you love? What practical steps have you taken to disentangle yourself from its negative effects on you or your loved ones?

3. Have you ever thought you were at a feast, only to find yourself in folly? How is sin often disguised as wonderful and refreshing?

4. What passions have pulled you away from Christ or have the potential to do so? For example, in what ways does idleness tempt you? Gossip?

5. In what ways are you a busybody instead of being busy for the body of Christ with the aim to glorify God?

6. How could you use 1 Corinthians 6:9–11 to help a new believer overcome their shame from their past addictions?

7. Do you know Christ's love for you, and do you love Christ? Do you serve Him as Lord and Savior? Do you trust Him with your life? Do you obey His commands? If you answered yes to these, how does your life display this reality? If you answered no, consider speaking with a Christian about any questions you may have regarding the faith.

8. How does knowing that Christ lived a life of obedience for you and took God's wrath on Himself on the cross of Calvary comfort, convict, or challenge you?

9. Seek to memorize Galatians 5:1 this week.

Part 2

The Fountain of Living Waters Has...

Carol got out her iPhone. When had she stopped constantly scrolling through social media and comparing herself to what she saw there? God had transformed her heart to thirst for the milk of God's Word instead of more technology.

Sarah stepped off the scale. When had the numbers lost their power over her? God had transformed her heart to thirst for spiritual health more than physical.

Gina drove past the mall parking lot. When had she stopped compulsively shopping? God had transformed her heart to thirst for the eternal rather than the temporal.

Amy laid her head down on her pillow. When had she stopped regularly engaging in sexual sin? God had transformed her heart to thirst for His love instead of the lusts of this world.

Lisa looked at her calendar. When had she stopped being so busy that there were now blank squares? God had transformed her heart to balance work with rest and worship.

Kay looked at her office wall. When had she stopped being anxious about failing in her career? God had transformed her heart to find her security and peace in him.

Tammy looked at her children. When had she stopped elevating motherhood to the detriment of other relationships and obligations? God had transformed her heart to see that her role of mother was one of several roles He had for her.

In part 1 of this book we learned that many women today are thirsting for springs of stagnant water that seem to temporarily quench their thirst but leave them, tragically, thirstier than when they began. In part 2 we will learn that Jesus offers us springs of living water that will transform our hearts and eternally satisfy our thirst. We will look at three main points: we have been washed with clean water, we have been given living water, and we have access to nourishing water.

Chapter 5

Clean Water

I like for things to be relatively neat and clean at my house. With four children, this is often hard to accomplish, but I still try. Oftentimes during the day I have to close my eyes to dirty fingerprints, muddy feet, food-stained mouths, and marker-stained fingers. Children like to explore their world, and it's often a messy process. But more than a clean house, I like for the people around me to have clean hearts. It would be easier that way, you know. Instead, I am a sinner living with five other sinners. That's a lot of sin in one house! Not only do I want the people around me to have a clean heart, but I want to have a clean heart too. I am painfully aware of the selfishness within me. I am far too quick to anger, criticism, envy, frustration, greed, irritation, manipulation, quarrels, and weariness in doing good to those around me. If a shower could cleanse sin, one a day wouldn't be enough for me. Thankfully, Jesus has come to clean us and set us free from slavery to sin and impure thirsts. In this chapter we'll learn how He does this, and why He does this.

Cleanliness Is Godliness

Ezekiel 36:25–27 says, "Then I will sprinkle clean water on you, and you shall be clean; I will cleanse you from all your filthiness and from all your idols. I will give you a new heart and put a new spirit within you; I will take the heart of stone out of your flesh and give you a heart of flesh. I will put My Spirit within you and cause you to walk in My statutes, and you will keep My judgments and do them." Ezekiel was prophesying during the exile, speaking messages of both judgment and grace. Here he was in the middle of one of the greatest messages of grace in the book. You have to recall a bit of Israel's sacrificial system to see the significance of these verses. If you were unclean in Israel, you were not welcome among God's people.

For example, in Leviticus we read, "Whoever of all your descendants throughout your generations, who goes near the holy things which the children of Israel dedicate to the LORD, while he has uncleanness upon him, that person shall be cut off from My presence: I am the LORD" (Lev. 22:3). But in Ezekiel we see that God has made His people clean from all their impurities and all their idols. Have you ever tried to scrub permanent marker off skin or clothing? It doesn't come off! The permanency of sin marks us; it cannot come off, no matter how hard we scrub. What we try to do with our own cleansing techniques and can never accomplish, God does for us. We can't take enough showers to wash away our sexual sin. We can't rinse with enough mouthwash to wash away the gossip, slander, or unkind words that come out of our mouths. We can't swim in deep enough waters to rid ourselves of the addictions we are enslaved to. But the good news of the gospel is that God not only can cleanse us but does cleanse us. Our salvation is not a possibility; it is a certainty.

Perhaps you need to be cleansed today, dear reader. Maybe you feel the shame of sexual sin. Perhaps you are worshiping someone or something other than Christ. Maybe your marriage and family life are filled with fighting. Perhaps your heart is pregnant with greed and envy. Maybe you are selfishly pursuing your own ambitions, always putting your own needs ahead of others' in order to get ahead in your career, ministry, or family plans. None of these things lead to the kingdom of God. They are ways of the flesh, not of the Spirit. We need God's mighty cleansing to free us from such things. Thankfully, not only does God cleanse us when we turn to Him in repentance and faith, but He also gives us a new heart.

A New Heart
When God saves us, He gives us a heart that beats for the things of Himself. He gives us a heart that longs for holiness and knowledge and righteousness. He gives us the Holy Spirit to cultivate godly fruit within us—love, joy, peace, longsuffering, kindness, goodness, faithfulness, gentleness, and self-control (Gal. 5:22–23). We cannot make our own hearts new. Left to us they will always be sick. We can't stop the sin that flows from them. But God can. He puts His Spirit within us so that we will walk in His ways.

A New Spirit

This new Spirit within us gives us power. The same power that raised Jesus Christ from the dead is the power within our hearts (Eph. 1:19–20). This is why Peter says, "His divine power has given to us all things that pertain to life and godliness" (2 Peter 1:3). Wow! Think about that for a moment. The Spirit within us is powerful enough to enable us to say no to the flesh and yes to the Spirit. That doesn't mean we will do so perfectly, but it means we no longer have to sin. We can truly say yes to Christ and no to the things of this world.

This is good news for women like Amy, who had become addicted to sexual sin. And it's good news for women like you and me. Our sin problem may or may not be sexual. It may be anger, envy, greed, gossip, idolatry, or love of money. Regardless of the specific sin, when we come to the Lord in repentance He washes us with clean water.

The Love of Christ

In Ephesians 5:25–27 we read, "Husbands, love your wives, just as Christ also loved the church and gave Himself for her, that He might sanctify and cleanse her with the washing of water by the word, that He might present her to Himself a glorious church, not having spot or wrinkle or any such thing, but that she should be holy and without blemish." In these verses Paul is writing to the church in Ephesus. He has taken the first half of the book to tell us the spiritual blessings we have in Christ. Now he calls Christians to respond to such grace. In other words, he grounds the imperative (what we are to do) in the indicative (what God has already done for us). These verses teach us that Christ loves us. He loves us so much that He laid down His life for us. Not just me, an individual, but us, God's people. It's a beautiful thing to recognize that we are part of the family of God. We are part of the covenant community. We are sisters in Christ.

This is good news for women like Carol, who constantly compare themselves to others they see on social media. Christ loves us as we are, but He loves us too much to leave us that way. In God's family there's no room for comparison. The cross is the great leveling ground. All of us come as sinners in need of a Savior.

It's also good news for women like Lisa, who keep their calendar overly full in an attempt to silence the loneliness they feel inside. These verses teach us that we are not alone. We are part of God's people that He is saving through the history of redemption. Our smaller story is just a piece of a far greater drama, with Christ as the hero of it all. In Ephesians 3:19 Paul prays that the saints will "know the love of Christ which passes knowledge; that you may be filled with all the fullness of God." Think of being filled with all the fullness of God! Because Christ has filled us with His love, we are freed from isolation into interdependence with the people of God. We no longer have to fill our calendars to try to silence the loneliness. We are part of the family of God!

These verses in Ephesians also teach us that Christ gave Himself up for us. We don't want to give ourselves up to anybody or anything. We are selfish at heart. We want comfort, control, and convenience. We want to guard our time and our resources, making sure nothing infringes on our schedule. We don't want to die to our own desires and passions. Instead, we want what we want when we want it. But Christ gave Himself up for us.

Why would He have done this? So that He might sanctify us. He has set us apart to be holy for God's glory. We are not our own but have been bought at a price (1 Cor. 6:20). He has saved us to sanctify us. How has He done this? By washing us with the water of the Word. This goes back to what we saw in Ezekiel. He makes us new creatures, setting us apart as His people. The Word of God transforms us, teaching us how we should live in God's presence as God's people. Again, why has Christ done this? So that He might present the church to Himself in the splendor of holiness. He has saved us from sin in order to sanctify us. He is making His bride ready for the great wedding day. But Jesus is not just our Bridegroom; He is also our Great High Priest.

A Great High Priest

The author of Hebrews says, "Having a High Priest over the house of God, let us draw near with a true heart in full assurance of faith, having our hearts sprinkled from an evil conscience and our bodies washed with pure water" (Heb. 10:21–22). Isn't this amazing? We have a Great High Priest over the house of God: Jesus Christ. He has given Himself as the final sacrifice in order to wash our hearts clean so that we can draw near to God with a true heart, in full assurance of faith.

In order to grasp the magnitude of this truth, we need to remember what we learned in the first section of this book. We learned how impure our thirsts are and how spiritually dead we are. How there is nothing in us that wants to draw near to God. How our hearts are deceitful above all things and desperately wicked. But here in these verses we see that Someone has done something amazing. Christ has made a way for us to draw near to God in full assurance of faith, with a true heart.

This is good news for our sister Gina, who had given her heart to shopping. She needed someone to pay a far greater debt than that which was on her credit card. She needed Jesus to wash her heart clean and give her a true heart that beat for the things of God. And so it is for you and me. We are far too easily satisfied with the stuff of shopping malls. Jesus wants to lift our eyes from the riches of this world to the riches of heaven and the riches that are ours in our Redeemer, Jesus Christ.

Spiritual Riches

What are these riches? We have been chosen in Christ before the foundation of the world (Eph. 1:4). Dwell for a moment on the concept of someone having their heart set on you from eternity past. Not because of any power, position, prestige, or possessions that you may have but simply out of love. It's mind-blowing. God the Father loved us and chose us as His children before the foundation of the world. We have been chosen in Christ in order to be changed (1:4). Apart from Christ we are unholy, but Christ changes our status to holy. Throughout our pilgrimage on this earth the Lord is progressively making us more and more Christlike. We have been adopted into God's family (1:5). No longer are we without a family. God is our Father, and we have a multitude of brothers and sisters from every tribe, tongue, and nation. We are trophies of God's grace (1:6).

None of us deserves to be saved. All of us were doomed to an eternity separated from God's love and fellowship. That He chose to save any of us is a demonstration of amazing grace. We are accepted in the Beloved (1:6). Let that sink in for a moment. I can't think of one woman who doesn't want to be accepted by others. Yet none of us would have had a chance to be accepted by God apart from His grace. We were unclean. There was no way of reconciliation apart from Christ. But in Christ we have His obedience and His atonement to make us presentable to the Father.

He does not only accept us; He also warmly welcomes us into His presence. We have redemption through His blood (1:7). His death accomplished our salvation. Therefore, our sins have been cast far away, and we are freed to love and obey Him. We have also obtained an inheritance (1:11). We look forward to the city that is to come where we will be with Christ, worshiping Him forever and working for His glory. Amazingly, we are also His inheritance. He loves us and longs for communion with His people (Deut. 4:20; 9:26, 29). Because He loves us, He is willing to make clean any and all who ask Him.

Christ Can Make Us Clean
Jesus had great multitudes following Him during His earthly ministry. Many placed their hope in His healing abilities. They were weary of suffering and heard of a Savior, so it's not hard to believe that many of them wanted to get close to Him. One day a leper came and

worshiped Him. People with leprosy were outcasts. Imagine an individual sitting in isolation within crowds of people, calling "Unclean, unclean," and you have a small glimpse into the loneliness a leper faced during his lifetime. But this leper had heard about Jesus, and he had heard enough to worship Him. His faith is evident in his trust: "Lord, if You are willing, You can make me clean" (Matt. 8:2).

The leper knew without a doubt that Jesus could cleanse him. The question was, would He? Would Jesus choose to heal him? I cannot imagine how this leper felt when he saw Jesus's hand coming toward him. How would you feel? Imagine having felt no touch for years. Everyone around you called you unclean. You'd been kept in isolation. But now someone reaches out and touches you. And not only this—Jesus's words accompanied His warmth. "I am willing; be cleansed" (Matt. 8:3). Wow! This is the kind of Savior we serve. One who is not only able but willing to cleanse us. Not only is He able to wash us with clean water, though; He also offers us living water, a topic we will look at in the next chapter.

Can you relate to my wanting a clean and neat house? Or clean and neat hearts around me? Or what about a clean heart within yourself? It is Christ alone who can cleanse. He is the only One who has clean hands and a pure heart. He is the only One who has not lifted up

His heart to an idol. And because He is clean, He can make us clean. Because He has been faithful, we can stand in God's presence. We will receive blessings from the Father because of our Lord and Savior Jesus Christ (see Ps. 24:3–6).

Thinking It Through

1. Describe a time when you have felt unclean because of sin.

2. In what ways have you tried to cleanse yourself from sin instead of trusting in Christ's work on your behalf?

3. If you're a Christian, how does it encourage you that you have a new heart and a new Spirit in Christ? If you're not a Christian, consider coming to Christ for cleansing today, and then share this good news with a Christian friend or pastor.

4. How could you use Ephesians 5:25–27 to help a friend understand Christ's love for her?

5. What does it mean that Christ is our Great High Priest? How could you teach this truth to someone under your leadership this week?

6. Think back through the spiritual riches discussed in this chapter. Which ones mean the most to you in your specific circumstances right now?

7. How could you use the story of the leper to help a friend struggling with whether God could ever forgive her for a particular sin?

8. Pray through Ephesians 1:3–14, thanking God for each one of the blessings you have received in Christ.

9. Seek to memorize Ephesians 1:3 today.

Chapter 6

Living Water

There is nothing like getting together with a dear friend after many years of not seeing each other and picking right up where you left off. Instead of spending time speaking about surface level things, you can jump straight into the struggles and joys in your heart at the moment. In many cases she knows your story, including your sin, suffering, shame, and service. In her presence you feel both known and loved.

I was speaking recently with a woman who was in the beginning of a dating relationship. As we conversed, I learned that the younger couple wasn't yet at the point of processing together issues that affected each other's hearts. It reminded me of those early days when my husband and I were still finding out things about each other, and how in every relationship you wonder what the other person is going to think about you when they find out your whole story.

Women long to be known and then loved when they are fully known. But there is only one person who will ever know us fully, and that is God. In this chapter we're going to learn that He knows every square inch of our story and still loves and pursues us in the midst of our sin and shame, our secrecy, and our suffering. In the midst of our dry and weary lands of anger or adultery, covetousness or catastrophe, depression or disillusionment, fights or failures, lust or longings, raging or recklessness, temptation or tears, He offers us living water that will lift us from the depths of despair and put us on our feet again so that we might tell others what He has done for us.

The Fountain of Living Waters

In the first section of this book we looked at Jeremiah 2:13 (see also 17:13):

> "For My people have committed two evils:
> They have forsaken Me, the fountain of
>   living waters,
> And hewn themselves cisterns—broken
>   cisterns that can hold no water."
> (Jer. 2:13)

We learned how fallen and fickle our hearts are. We learned how quickly we turn from the Fountain of living water and drink muddy, murky water. After Jeremiah, the prophet Zechariah, in prophesying about the coming day of the Lord after the exile, declared "that living waters shall flow from Jerusalem" (Zech. 14:8). Jerusalem symbolized God's presence, promises, and protection. This imagery of the Lord God as the Fountain of living waters is picked up in the New Testament in the Gospel of John.

An Unlikely Meeting

In John 4:1–9 we learn that Jesus left Judea and returned to Galilee. In order to get there, He had to pass through Samaria. During His travel through Samaria He came to the town of Sychar. This town was near the field that Jacob had given to Joseph, and Jacob's well was there. Jesus was very tired from His journey. Around noon, He sat down beside Jacob's well. While He was sitting there a Samaritan woman came to draw water. Since His disciples were away in the city buying food, Jesus asked this woman for a drink of water. But since Jews didn't ordinarily deal with Samaritans, she questioned why He, a Jew, would ask her, a Samaritan woman, for a drink of water.

Let's pause for a moment because there are three unlikely things going on in this passage—unlikely, that is, from a human perspective, for, as we shall see, this was a divine appointment. First, a Jew was traveling through Samaria. Jews and Samaritans were not friends. The Samaritans had their own version of the Pentateuch and their own place of worship, and many of them had a mixed ancestry (part Jew and part Gentile). Strict Jews avoided traveling through Samaria altogether so as not to become defiled by people they considered unclean. So it is noteworthy that Jesus was in Samaria and resting at this well.

Second, a woman from Samaria came to draw water at noon. Women didn't normally draw water at noon. They drew water in the morning or the evening when it was cooler. But this woman didn't want to be in the company of other women because she was ashamed of her sexual immorality. So she came at a time when she thought she would be alone and anonymous.

Finally, Jesus, a Jew, asked a Samaritan woman for a drink. Remember that Jews had no dealings with Samaritans, and here not only was Jesus asking a Samaritan for a drink, but He was asking a *woman* for a drink at a time when His disciples were away in the city buying food. Jewish men did not deal with Samaritan women. Within one generation of Jesus's meeting with this woman, the Jewish leaders implemented a law "that reflected long-standing popular sentiment, to the effect that all 'the daughters of the Samaritans are menstruants from their cradle' and therefore perpetually in a state of ceremonial uncleanness."[1] Furthermore, remember the reputation this woman had. Here was Jesus, alone with this sexually immoral woman in the heat of the day at a well in Samaria. With these things in mind, let's continue seeing how this story unfolds.

An Unlikely Mistake
In John 4:10–15 we learn of further dialogue between Jesus and this Samaritan woman. Jesus answered the woman's question with "If you knew the gift of God, and who it is who says to you, 'Give Me a drink,' you would have asked Him, and He would have given you living water" (4:10). The woman was surprised because clearly Jesus had nothing to draw water with, and the well was deep. She wondered where He would get this living water

---

1. D. A. Carson, *The Gospel According to John*, The Pillar New Testament Commentary (Grand Rapids: Eerdmans, 1991), 217–18.

about which He was speaking. She questioned if He was greater than their father Jacob, who, along with his sons and livestock, had drunk from that well and later given it to them. Jesus told her that whoever drank of Jacob's water would be thirsty again, but whoever drinks His water will never thirst again. In fact, the water He gives becomes a fountain of water that springs up into eternal life. The Samaritan woman replied with a request for His living water so that she would not thirst or need to come there again and draw water.

Let's pause for a minute. What is going on here? Jesus is not asking this woman for a drink of water at all. Instead, Jesus wants to give her a drink of water— a drink of living water. Understandably, she's confused. There's nothing in His hand that leads her to believe He can draw water, yet His confidence also leads her to believe that it's unlikely He is mistaken in what He's saying. And she is loyal to father Jacob, so she wouldn't have expected someone greater than Jacob to be talking with her. And yet Jesus is so persistent, and so clear, and so inviting in calling her to drink of His living water that will lead to eternal life. She recognizes what a gift He is offering her and says, "Give me this water so that I will not be thirsty or have to come here again."

Think of Kay, who was surrounded by signs of achievement but still filled with anxiety. What she had thought would lead to security had led to insecurity. Listen to her imploring, "Give me this water so that I will not be thirsty or have to keep meeting the next deadline, hoping I will measure up once again."

Or think of Tammy, who has poured so much into her children. She is weary and for the first time realizes that what she had thought would fulfill her has left her feeling frazzled. Just listen to her saying, "Give me this water so that I can stop running in every different direction for carpool destinations, shopping malls, sports games, lessons, and recitals, never stopping for anything or anyone else."

Or think of your own circumstances. Don't you long to say in your hardest, weakest, most tempting moments, "Give me this water so that I can stop trying to do life on my own, thinking my plans and purposes are best, thinking my own water will satisfy"?

But wait. There seems to have been a threat to the woman's thirst finally being quenched. In verses 16–26 Jesus told her to go and call her husband. When the woman told Jesus that she had no husband, Jesus affirmed that her response was accurate. And He went on to tell her that she'd had five husbands, and that the man she was living with at the current time wasn't her husband. The woman perceived that Jesus was a prophet and told Him that the Samaritans had worshiped on Mount Gerizim, while the Jews worshiped in Jerusalem. Jesus replied that an hour was coming, and was already present, when true worshipers would worship the Father. He told her that salvation was of the Jews and that true worshipers would worship the Father in spirit and in truth because the Father was seeking such worshipers. Since God is a spirit, His worshipers must worship Him in spirit and truth. The Samaritan woman declared her belief in the coming Messiah, to which Jesus responded, "I who speak to you am He" (4:26).

This woman must have felt undone when Jesus told her to go and call her husband. I'm sure she thought the offer for living water was off the table. She probably wanted to crawl away from the well and not engage in conversation with this man any longer as shame filled her heart. And then, as He revealed that He knew her past, surely she must have thought that there was no way she had a chance of drinking this water He had offered. But instead, Jesus told her the gospel. Salvation was from the Jews (and He Himself was the Jew of whom He spoke!). He was the Prophet of all prophets. The Father is seeking worshipers to worship Him in spirit and in truth. And He invited her to be one of them. But that's not all. Let's finish the story.

An Unlikely Message
In John 4:27–30 we learn that the disciples returned from getting food in town and marveled that Jesus was talking with a woman. Yet not one of them questioned Him. The woman left her water jar, went into town, and summoned the people, "Come, see a Man who told me all things that I ever did. Could this be the Christ?" (4:29). Then the townspeople left the city to go to Jesus.

This story began with three unlikely events. Now it closes with two more.

First, the disciples did not question the Samaritan woman or Jesus. Don't you just know how badly they wanted to ask questions! This situation was unheard of, but they refrained from speaking. Surely they trusted

Jesus, and their trust silenced the voicing of their inquis-
itive thoughts. Second, this woman, who wanted to be
alone at the well in her shame, went into town and called
the people to come and see Christ. How unlikely this
was! Shame drives us to secrecy and isolation, but the
Savior drives us to confess our sin, and then His name,
and to invite others to do so as well.

The heart that has drunk living water is a heart filled
with worship that leads to witness. When we have met
Jesus and experienced His living water, we will cry out
in worship of Him and want to show Him to others. The
unlikely events of this story point to the most unlikely
event in history: God became flesh and dwelt among
us (John 1:14), revealing His glory. Jesus lived a life of
perfect obedience for us and died a cursed death that
turned God's wrath away from us so that you and I might
live forever. The glorious truth of the gospel is that God
has done something seemingly scandalous—died for
sinners like you and me—so that we might live forever.

So, I have to ask you, dear reader, Do you love Jesus?
Does your heart overflow with thanksgiving for the living
water He has given to you? Do you worship Him alone?
And do you long to tell others about Him?

If Anyone Thirsts
In John 7 we learn that during the Jewish Feast of Taber-
nacles Jesus made His way into the city of Jerusalem. On
the last and climactic day of the great feast, Jesus stood
up and made an astonishing offer: "If anyone thirsts, let
him come to Me and drink. He who believes in Me, as
the Scripture has said, out of his heart will flow rivers

of living water" (7:37–38). What the prophet Isaiah had declared, "With joy you will draw water from the wells of salvation" (Isa. 12:3) and, "Ho! Everyone who thirsts, come to the waters" (Isa. 55:1), Jesus was fulfilling. He was announcing that He is God, and that whoever believes in Him will receive the Holy Spirit.

When the Holy Spirit inhabits the hearts of believers, the power and presence of the living God are at work in those hearts in such a way that it's as though rivers of living water were pouring forth from them. This isn't true only for some elite group of believers. This is true for every believer. We have the power and presence of God within our hearts, reminding us of His promises. That's something to be excited about! But just as in Jesus's day, so in ours, different people respond differently. Some think He was just a prophet. Some think He was a lunatic. Some think Christians have been deceived into believing a lie. But Scripture is clear. This Jesus is the Christ, the Son of the living God (Matt. 16:16), and what we do with Him matters for all of eternity.

Living Fountains of Water

In Revelation 7:15–17 the apostle John speaks of believers before the throne of God, serving Him in His presence. Because of Him they no longer hunger and thirst. And the Lamb is in the midst of the throne, shepherding believers and leading them to fountains of living waters. This imagery of living waters is picked up at the end of the book of Revelation in the description of the new heaven and the new earth, specifically the river of life flowing through the new Jerusalem (Rev. 22:1–2).

In both of these passages we learn that the springs of
living water Jesus offers are more wonderful than anything we've ever imagined. The world offers us all kinds
of springs—the springs of achievement, beauty, career,
drugs and alcohol, food, power, popularity, materialism,
and entertainment, among others—but these all fuel
our thirst for more because they never satisfy. We think
that if we just drink a little bit more of the things of this
world we'll be fulfilled, but all the while we're having
a feast in the grave (see Prov. 9:13–18). There is something vastly different about the springs of living water
that Jesus leads us to. He's WITH us.

First, God's presence is there. The crux of God's covenant is "I will…be your God and you shall be My people"
(Lev. 26:12). When we come to saving faith, God's Holy
Spirit takes up residence in our hearts. God is with us.
One day we will be with Jesus in the new heaven and the
new earth, but even now He is with us by His Spirit. His
presence never leaves us.

Second, God's comfort is there. The Holy Spirit is
our comforter. In the midst of suffering on this side of
glory God comforts us. We don't have to turn to comfort
foods, comfort malls, or comfort drinks; we have Christ.
In the middle of the valley of the shadow of death, He
comforts us in our grief and suffering. He carries us
through floods and fires, fights and frustrations, fall-
enness and fickleness. As the psalmist says, "He turns a
wilderness into pools of water, and dry land into water-
springs" (Ps. 107:35).

Third, God's protection is there. We are not promised physical protection on this side of glory, but spiritual

protection. Humans and evil spiritual forces cannot ultimately harm those who are in Christ. We don't have to fear for our lives or the lives of our loved ones. God protects His children and has numbered our days (Pss. 121; 139:16). When we are overcome with anxiety, we can turn to the Almighty and rest in Him, our fortress and deliverer.

Finally, God's sustenance is there. Think about the biggest meal you've ever enjoyed. I'm sure you thought to yourself, "I don't ever want to eat again." But later you found yourself hungry for more. This is not the case with God's sustenance. God quenches our thirst and satisfies our hunger forever. Our palates are far too easily pleased with the platters of this world, when all the while we have the person of Jesus Christ offering to pour us living water. He is waiting. He is willing. And He is watching. Dear reader, why don't you walk away from that empty spring to His fountain? His presence is there; His comfort is there; His protection is there; and His sustenance is there. Your thirst will be quenched as it's never been quenched before.

So far in part 2 of this book, we've learned that the Fountain of living waters has washed us with clean water and has given us living water. In the next chapter we will learn that He has also given us access to nourishing water.

Where are you at today in your heart? Are you secretly slouching to the well at noon when nobody will see you? Are you longing for a friend who will love you even when they know everything about you? Jesus not only cares, but He comes and offers you living water to quench your thirst and set you free to live for Him.

Thinking It Through

1. How does it make you feel that God knows every square inch of you, and why do you feel that way?

2. How does the unlikely meeting between Jesus and the Samaritan woman encourage you?

3. How are you relieved by this story when you think of your own life?

4. How does the Samaritan woman's witness encourage you to go and tell others about Christ?

5. How could you use the story of the Samaritan woman to share the gospel with an unbeliever?

6. How does it encourage you that you have God's power and presence within you by the Holy Spirit's indwelling?

7. What kind of worldly springs are you already drinking from or are tempted to drink from today?

8. How will you exchange your worldly spring for the Fountain of living waters?

9. Seek to memorize John 4:13–14 this week.

Chapter 7

Nourishing Water

As a mom of four children, I have certainly read my share of books or articles on nutrition. I wanted to make sure I was nourishing my children well. Whether it was breastfeeding in the early years, nonprocessed foods in the toddler years, or nutritious meals as we embarked upon the teenage years, I was concerned about nourishing my children so that they would grow properly. Sadly, the obsession our culture has with clean foods, and the concern mothers often have with nourishing foods for their children, isn't matched by an obsession with nourishing our children on God's Word. Yet it should be. Malnutrition of Scripture is far more dangerous than malnutrition of food.

A Tree Planted by Streams of Water

Psalm 1:1–3 teaches us that the blessed man or woman is the one who doesn't walk in ungodly counsel, or among sinners and scorners, but instead delights in the law of the Lord, meditating on it day and night, with the result of fruitfulness. Just as a tree planted by rivers of water brings forth delightful fruit each season, so too the godly woman planted in the Word of God proves to be fruitful in her words and works. Since God has chosen to reveal Himself through His Word, it is both necessary and a privilege to meditate on it day and night. Yet we are far too easily distracted with the things in this world that promise to nourish us.

Think about food, for example. How many countless hours do we spend thinking about food? Food is a wonderful thing, and very nourishing. But oftentimes food becomes an idol in our lives. We can try to avoid food in order to stay skinny, or we can binge on food and then purge it, or we can overindulge in food and put on extra pounds our body doesn't need. Or what about beauty? How many countless hours do we spend in front of the mirror? There's nothing wrong with looking nice, but we can easily take this to the excess and spend more time on our external beauty than we do cultivating internal beauty in the Word of God and prayer. Or think of exercise. How many hours do we spend working out? Again, exercise is very beneficial and oftentimes enjoyable. But too many times it becomes an activity we rely on in order to feel good about ourselves. So none of these (food, beauty, and exercise) are bad in and of themselves, but too often they replace the time we spend in the Word of God, leaving us withered, drained, fruitless, and exhausted instead of fruitful and full of joy.

Waters of Rest

Psalm 23 has become so familiar to many of us that we've lost the wonder of the truth it teaches. Read the first two verses slowly and out loud:

> The LORD is my shepherd;
> I shall not want.
> He makes me to lie down in green pastures;
> He leads me beside the still waters.
> He restores my soul;
> He leads me in the paths of righteousness
> For His name's sake.

These verses point us to the good shepherd, Jesus Christ. As the good shepherd, He knows God's people by name and has willingly laid down His life for them (John 10:14–15). I have never known a woman who doesn't want to be known by name by her leader. Because Christ is our good shepherd, we need not want anything else but Him. Christ is enough for us to be completely content.

As our good shepherd, He also leads us through green pastures and beside waters of rest. No woman has ever told me, "I have too much time to rest." The women I know lead very busy lives and crave rest. Whether they are young or old, single or married, working in a career or raising children at home, they have lists of things they need to do and lines of people for whom they need to care. Some of them are on the verge of depression because they feel overwhelmed by how much they have to do and how many people they have to serve. So these verses are refreshing for our weary souls.

Jesus invites us to come to Him for true rest (Matt. 11:28–30). In Him we can lay down our burdens and take up His yoke of rest. Since we are called to work six days and rest one day, this truth doesn't mean we're going to be on vacation the rest of our lives. But it does mean we can stop being busybodies and be busy about our Father's business, trusting Him to lead us in right paths that are at the same time restful. Too often we are busy in order to perform. God calls us to rest in His Son's perfect performance on our behalf and then get busy for His kingdom purposes.

As our good shepherd, He also restores our souls, making sinners righteous. He knows us by name, saves us from our sin and shame, and gives us a new name (saint). In Christ we are set apart to be holy ones for His glory. He enables us by His Spirit to walk in the way of righteousness for His name's sake. Our lives are to glorify Him, and as we glorify Him, we will enjoy our shepherd's lovingkindness that leads us through still waters. We cannot enjoy our shepherd, though, if we don't know Him, and the way we know our shepherd is by studying Scripture.

Cultivating a Love for God's Word
In 2 Timothy 3:14–17 Paul gives a charge to Timothy:

> Continue in the things which you have learned and been assured of, knowing from whom you have learned them, and that from childhood you have known the Holy Scriptures, which are able to make you wise for salvation through faith which is in Christ Jesus.

All Scripture is given by inspiration of God, and is profitable for doctrine, for reproof, for correction, for instruction in righteousness, that the man of God may be complete, thoroughly equipped for every good work.

I think one of the deepest tragedies occurring in the church today is that we have more readily available access to Bibles and Bible resources than any generation before us but yet are an increasingly illiterate people when it comes to Bible knowledge. Perhaps it's the fact that it is so readily available to us that we assume it will always be there in the future and don't put a high priority on seizing the opportunity to study it in the present. Or maybe we've become too busy with the things of this world to take the time to be women of the Word. Whatever the explanation, Paul's words are important here for several reasons.

First, he calls Timothy to continue in what he has learned and firmly believed from childhood. We know from the first chapter in 2 Timothy that he learned it from his mother and grandmother, which is a tremendous encouragement to us to instill the faith in our children, grandchildren, and the covenant children in our churches. Our thirst matters for the next generation. We either train our children, grandchildren, and the covenant children in our churches to thirst for the things of this world or we teach them to thirst for the things of eternity.

Lois and Eunice taught Timothy to thirst for the things of eternity. But in Judges 2:7–10 we learn that this is not always the case. During the days of Joshua,

God's people faithfully served Him. Even the elders who outlived Joshua continued to faithfully serve the Lord because they'd seen His great works. But after Joshua's generation died out, there arose another generation who didn't know the Lord or the works He had accomplished. Stop and ponder that for a moment. An entire generation missed being trained in the words and works of the Lord. How tragic.

This leads us to examine our own lives. What are we doing to instill the truths of the faith in the next generation? How are we encouraging them to memorize Scripture? How are we purposefully training our children in catechism questions and answers to give them categories to think about biblical truths? How often do we seize moments of discipline and disciple them in the truths of the gospel? How do we talk about eternal things when we have their attention? When do we set aside time to meet with them to talk about what is going on in their lives and bring God's wisdom from His Word to bear on the situation? If we're not actively teaching them biblical truths, we are missing the opportunity to pass the faith to the next generation, and the results will be disastrous. Remember the results in Israel? As the curtain closes on the gruesome stories in the book of Judges, the final verse reads, "In those days there was no king in Israel; everyone did what was right in his own eyes" (Judg. 21:25). We cannot save our children, but we can teach them truth that by God's grace will take root in their hearts and bear fruit. Let's not grow weary in talking about the Word wherever we go and whenever we can.

Second, Paul teaches us that Scripture is able to make us wise for salvation through faith in Christ (2 Tim. 3:15). In a world that teaches us myriad ways to save ourselves, we need the wisdom of Scripture teaching us that it is Christ alone who saves. And we will need to be prepared when others ask us the reason for our hope in Christ alone (1 Peter 3:15). I had the opportunity to share my hope of salvation in Christ alone as I was returning from a speaking engagement in South America. Seated next to me on the plane was a man who was Roman Catholic, and beside him was his daughter, who had also grown up Roman Catholic but who had since diverged from her father's more conservative views. Since the man asked me what I was doing in South America, I was able to share the gospel with him in my reply. I made it very clear that the Bible teaches that we are not saved by our good works but by Christ alone. He argued against this point, insisting that good works save us. Again, I assured him that I was not a good girl, could not save myself by my good works, and needed Christ. Later in the flight I offered him my lunch from the airline. He said, "See! You just did a good work." I chuckled and replied, "Yes, but the only reason I could do that is because of God's grace at work within me." I have no way of knowing how my words that day impacted him. But I was grateful the Lord gave me the opportunity to proclaim that we are saved by grace alone, through faith alone in Christ alone.

Third, Scripture is God's Word to us. He has revealed Himself to us in order to nourish our souls. Through it He teaches us, reproves us, corrects us, and trains us in righteousness. Think of the greatest teacher you've ever had and the greatest teaching you've ever received. Christ is a far superior teacher, and Scripture is far greater teaching. Think about the hardest-hitting reproof you've ever received. Scripture is a far more accurate diagnosis than any you've received from this world. Think about the most impactful correction you've ever received. The Bible is far better at correcting our way when we are off the path. Or think about the best trainer you've ever had and the best training you've ever received. Christ is far greater and the Word far better able to train us for righteous living. For this reason we should submerse ourselves in study of it.[1]

Finally, the study of Scripture results in a life that is competent and equipped for every good work. Who doesn't want to be competent? We spend thousands of dollars on education so that we can be competent in our fields. Yet too often we neglect the Word of God on our way up the educational ladder. Or who doesn't want to be equipped? Think of how many hours we often pour into internships to be equipped for our careers. Yet how often do we pour those same hours into the study of Scripture?

A Light in a Dark Place
Not only Paul but also Peter reminds us that we do well to pay attention to the Word of God. In 2 Peter 1:19–21 Peter says,

---

1. If you're looking for a Bible study that is gospel centered, see my studies on the books of Judges and Ruth; Ezra and Nehemiah; Romans; Hebrews; 1 Peter, 2 Peter, and Jude; and Revelation. See the bibliography for details.

And so we have the prophetic word confirmed, which you do well to heed as a light that shines in a dark place, until the day dawns and the morning star rises in our hearts;

Knowing this first, that no prophecy of Scripture is of any private interpretation, for prophecy never came by the will of man, but holy men of God spoke as they were moved by the Holy Spirit.

The Word of God is like a light shining in a dark place. It shines into the darkness of our own souls, convicting us of sin. It shines into the darkness of our suffering, comforting us when we feel as though we can't go on. It shines into the weariness we may have in service, encouraging us to be faithful even when we are tired. Apart from Christ we don't want anything to do with this light. But in Christ we are able to truly love the light, and although it can be painful to have God's light illumine the darkness of our hearts, it produces godly fruit.

Think of Amy. The reason she was able to turn away from sexual sin is that God graciously revealed His love for her. He replaced her taste for the false loves of this world with a taste for the greatest story ever told—the story of His Son found in Scripture. The same is true for you and me. God's light is gracious. It lovingly reveals our darkness and draws us out of sin into holiness. As we yield to the light of the Holy Spirit, we crucify the desires of our flesh and cling to the delights of our relationship with our Father. Such light is like nourishing water to our souls. How should we respond to such nourishing water?

Fearing the Lord and Focusing Our Desires on His Word

In Psalm 19:7–11 David tells us six things about Scripture. First, it is perfect (v. 7). We don't have to look any further for refreshment as we walk in the wilderness of this world. Scripture is our sole sustenance. It tells us everything we need to know about God and ourselves. It tells us the grand story of salvation, including creation, the fall, redemption, and consummation. It is a mirror that shows us our sin and our need of a Savior and has the power to convert our souls.

Second, it is sure (v. 7). We don't have to have the highest level of education and see the top-rated counselor. God's Word is our steady and sure guide through all of life. Although it does not contain specific answers in terms of which college to attend, which job to take, which man to marry, how many children to have, how to plan our financial future, and the like, it gives us the wisdom we need to make godly decisions in each of these different areas.

Third, it is right (v. 8). Our hearts are often saturated with suffering on this side of glory, but God's Word makes straight paths for our feet in the midst of it. Our hearts can continually rejoice in His trustworthiness. We don't need to doubt His goodness, love, or faithfulness. There's no need to put God to the test. He's perfectly dependable.

Fourth, it is pure (v. 8). In a world that wants to turn our eyes to worthless things, Scripture gives us an alternative. It opens our eyes to see things clearly. Those things that look so alluring to us when we're out of the Word become alarming to us when we're in it. Those things that feel so right to us when we're in the world feel so wrong to us when we're in the Word. Those things that taste so good to us when we're around bad company taste so bad to us when we're in the presence of God.

Fifth, it is clean (v. 9). In the wake of sin, we can't scrub ourselves hard enough to get it off. Scripture tells us how we can really be clean. Christ has cleansed us by the washing of water with the Word (Eph. 5:26). Forget the shower or the tub. The Word of God is like a flower opening up truth to you that is fragrant enough to feed your soul.

Finally, it is true and righteous (v. 9). In a world that promotes lies, it is a comfort to know that Scripture contains absolute truth. Such truth tastes better than honey and trumps the treasures of this world. Revelation is not to be ignored, but stored in our hearts. The two roads from which we choose, the way of the righteous or the way of the rebellious, have very different ends. The way of the rebellious ends in eternal separation from the Creator and Redeemer. The way of the righteous ends in eternal communion with him. Our thirst matters for all eternity.

Christ is the Word that became flesh and dwelt among humankind to reveal God's glory (John 1:14). He is perfect, sure, right, pure, clean, true, and our greatest treasure. As those who are in the living Word, we are to devote a great deal of time and attention to the written Word. We cannot walk the road of righteousness apart from it. It will revive us on our journey, give us wisdom in our peril, rejoice our hearts in our suffering, enlighten our eyes in the midst of our temptations, be our constant companion in our lives, and keep us immersed in right thinking, so that we don't succumb to the sweets of this world but stay steadfast in the sweetness of Scripture that shows us our Savior.

◆ ◆ ◆ ◆

How well nourished are you when it comes to Scripture? Are you anemic in terms of the nutrition offered in the Bible? Are you starved for truth? What about your children? Are you feeding them nutritious truths from Scripture daily, or are they starving in a house full of food? Christ is the great nourisher, and we have the privilege to partake of the food of His Word. What are we waiting for? It's time to dig in!

As we close this chapter, as well as this second part of the book, let's remember Carol, Sarah, Gina, Amy, Lisa, Kay, and Tammy. They have been washed with clean water, been given living water, and accessed nourishing water. That is my prayer for you, dear reader. Whatever thirst has ensnared you in your past, Jesus offers to wash you with clean water, give you living water, and provide you with nourishing water.

Thinking It Through

1. How could you help a friend understand the importance of feeding on the Word of God by comparing it to feeding on nutritious food? What Scripture passages could you use? For example, Psalm 19:10 tells us that God's precepts are "sweeter also than honey and the honeycomb."

2. In what ways are you withered, drained, fruitless, and exhausted instead of fruitful and full of joy? What does Psalm 1:1–3 instruct you to do?

3. Spend time in prayer, confessing the areas you listed above in which you are fruitless and lacking in joy, along with the reasons why. Cry out to your heavenly Father, asking Him to fill you with joy and help you to bear much fruit through your work for His glory.

4. What did you learn in this chapter about Jesus being our shepherd, and how did these truths comfort you?

5. In what ways are you cultivating a love for God's Word in your own heart? In the hearts of those you lead?

6. From Psalm 19:7–11, what six things do you learn about Scripture?

7. How has this chapter encouraged you to access nourishing water from God's Word? How do you plan to make the time to do this?

8. Seek to memorize Psalm 1:1–3 this week.

Part 3

We Respond By...

Carol had a hard time focusing on her work and was tempted to scroll through social media posts, comparing herself to what she saw.

Sarah had gotten a low grade on a paper in graduate school and was tempted to drown her woes in exercise.

Gina had a tough week at work and was tempted once again to shop her stress away.

Amy was having trouble in relationships again and was tempted to escape into sexual sin.

Lisa was lonelier than ever and was tempted to fill her calendar with needless activities in an attempt to numb her pain.

Kay had received a blow from her boss and was tempted to believe she was a failure.

And Tammy's children were doing so well in school and sports that she was tempted to give everything she had to help them succeed even more.

Each one of these women had realized that becoming a follower of Christ didn't mean leaving temptation behind. In fact, they were much more aware than before of the struggle between what they knew they should do for the Lord and what their flesh wanted to do. They were recognizing the battle they were in and the necessity of both thirsting for and drinking from springs of deep water that would help them say no to the world, the flesh, and the devil and yes to Christ.

In this book so far we have learned that many women today are thirsting for springs of stagnant water that seem to temporarily quench their thirst but leave them thirstier than when they began. This is tragic. Jesus offers us springs of living water that will transform our hearts and eternally satisfy our thirst. In this third section we will learn that this living water results in a fruitful life that glorifies God by our loving, enjoying, trusting, and obeying Him.[1] Although these four can't be separated from one another, they can be distinguished from each other. So I want us to look at some passages of Scripture in the next two chapters to help us learn what it means to glorify God in each one of these ways.

---

1. New City Catechism, A. 6. See also Deut. 11:1.

Chapter 8

Loving and Enjoying God

Have you ever had one of those moments when you looked at your husband and children and realized you had stopped loving and enjoying them as you once had? The mundane moments of life had long since replaced the mountaintop experiences. Suffering seemed to hide what had once been smiles. Sin eroded what could have been edifying and encouraging moments. Petty arguments, furrowed brows, temper tantrums, and the like seemed to have taken over the home. You didn't know exactly how you had gotten there, but you knew you needed counsel. You knew something had to change, or the family ship was going to sink, and you were going down with it. Or maybe things aren't quite that bad yet, but deep down you feel dissatisfied. Maybe you're bored with the monotonous routine in which you find yourself week after week. Perhaps what you once thought your life would look like at your age and season of life hasn't materialized at all, and you feel discouraged and depressed.

It's really no mystery what has happened to us. Scripture tells us that we're selfish sinners living for our own pleasures, thirsting for the things of this world—adulteresses who have turned to other lovers to meet our so-called needs (James 4:1–4). Thankfully, Scripture also tells us the solution. We need to humble ourselves before God, cry out for help, and recognize that He gives grace for each moment (4:6). Somewhere along the way we stopped working at our marriage and family life and unknowingly started drifting apart. We stopped the hard work of loving with our actions and scheduling time with our family members so that we could enjoy them.

I was reminded of how easily this happens one Saturday when our family was kayaking. After paddling my way around the lake, I stopped to rest my arms for a minute. All of a sudden I felt branches in my hair. I turned and realized that I had drifted into a tree that hung over the lake and was at the shore. As I quickly paddled back out into the middle of the lake, I thought about how easily we drift in terms of our intimacy with Christ when we start coasting in our relationship with Him. How many times have you heard people talk about the beginning of their relationship with Christ more than about their present relationship with Him? It's as though the best days of the relationship were behind them.

And oftentimes that's true. If we're not purposeful in loving and enjoying God, we will begin drifting away from Him instead of toward Him. Relationships take work. We have to be intentional in spending time with another person and cultivating a godly relationship with them. It's no different with the Lord. He has given us the means of grace to know Him—the Bible, prayer, and the sacraments (baptism and the Lord's Supper)—but we still have to open our Bible, pour out our hearts in prayer, and drive to the local church and engage in worship. James says that faith without works is a dead faith (James 2:26).

In the previous section of this book, we looked at what Christ has done for us. Now we want to look at how we should respond to Him in a way that glorifies His holy name. We will begin with what it means to love Him.

God First Loved Us

One of the ways in which we glorify God is by loving Him. But before we ask what it means to love God, we need to start with the profound truth that God first loved us. In fact, it is only because God first loved us that we are able, by His enabling power, to now love Him. God has displayed His love for us in many ways. First, He has initiated a relationship with us so that He can be present with us. This relationship is called a covenant, which I have defined elsewhere as *God's sovereign initiation to have a binding relationship with His people, grounded in His grace and promises, and secured by His own blood.*[1]

Think through Scripture and consider all the times God met with His people. To name just a few examples, He met with Adam and Eve in the garden of Eden, with Moses at the burning bush, with Israel at Mount Sinai, with David in David's house (2 Sam. 7:18), and with Solomon at Gibeon in a dream (1 Kings 3:5). When we

---

1. Sarah Ivill, *The Covenantal Life: Appreciating the Beauty of Theology and Community* (Grand Rapids: Reformation Heritage Books, 2018), 5.

come to the New Testament, God dwells with His people through His Son, Jesus Christ. Jesus met with several people during His earthly ministry to show that He loved them. Think about His time with Mary, Martha, and Lazarus. He ate meals with them and raised Lazarus from the dead (John 11:1–44). Or the time He met with Peter by the Sea of Galilee. Peter had denied Him three times, yet Jesus gave Him a second chance to reaffirm His love and devotion to Him (John 21:15–19). Yes, God has shown us how much He loves us by being present with us. But this is not all.

God has also shown us that He loves us by sending His Son to save His people. John 3:16 is so familiar to our ears that I fear we've forgotten the grandness of its truth. Slow down and read it out loud: "For God so loved the world that He gave His only begotten Son, that whoever believes in Him should not perish but have everlasting life." The Lord God didn't have to save any of us. We all deserve to be condemned. But in His grace and mercy He chose a people for Himself before the foundation of the world, that we might be holy and blameless before Him (Col. 1:22). His love doesn't just extend to our initial salvation from sin, death, and the devil, but to our complete sanctification. He is progressively making us more like Jesus, a process that will be completed upon Christ's return.

Don't miss the good news that God's love does not depend on us. We are terrible lovers. Our hearts are turned away from God. We are adulteresses at heart (James 4:4). Moses told Israel that the Lord didn't set His love on them because they were the greatest of peoples but because He loved them and is faithful to the covenant He made with Abraham and renewed with Isaac and Jacob (Deut. 7:7–9). Because He has loved us, we are to love Him. But how do we love Him?

Mary's Love for Jesus

In John 12:1–8 we learn that six days before the final Passover Jesus would enjoy with His disciples before His death, Jesus visited the town of Bethany. Bethany was the place where Jesus had raised Lazarus from the dead. While He was there, Mary, Martha, and Lazarus had Jesus to supper. Martha served, Lazarus sat at the table with Jesus, and Mary anointed Jesus's feet with very costly and fragrant oil, wiping them with her hair. One of His disciples, Judas Iscariot, who would later betray Jesus, questioned why the oil wasn't sold for money that could be given to the poor. He didn't really have any concern for the poor, but he was a thief and could have stolen the money gained from the sale. Jesus replied to Judas, "Let her alone; she has kept this for the day of My burial. For the poor you have with you always, but Me you do not have always" (John 12:7–8). There are several things to notice in these verses.

First, Mary recognized whom she had in the person of Jesus Christ. In the previous chapter we learn what Mary said to Jesus after Lazarus had died and before Jesus raised him from the dead. She said very clearly and with conviction, "Lord, if You had been here, my brother would not have died" (John 11:32). Mary knew that Jesus was God and therefore had the power to keep Lazarus from dying. Now, six days before Jesus's final Passover before His death, Mary anoints Jesus with perfume.

Second, Mary recognized who she was as a sinner in desperate need of grace. She put herself in the posture of a lowly and humble servant, stooping down and untying her hair to anoint her Savior's feet. This was her home. She was one of the hosts. But she recognized that her guest, God the Son, was far greater than she was.

Third, Jesus acknowledged Mary's love. He received Mary's act of devotion and defended her against Judas's criticism. There was no "Put it away, Mary" or "Save it for the poor" or "I'm not worthy of such love." No, Jesus knew that Mary's act of love was a profession of faith in Him as the Son of God and a proclamation of her love for Him. And He accepted it.

This story is startling and convicting. How often do we recognize whom we have in Christ? He left His Father's side for us. He promised redemption for us. He walked perfectly in our place the whole time He lived on this earth, so that His obedience might be counted as our obedience. He died in our place on the cross, so that His death might take the place of our having to bear the curse of God. We should gaze in wonder at our Savior, recognizing the enormous sacrifice He made to accomplish our redemption and expressing our utmost devotion to Him.

The problem is that we often fail to recognize just how sinful we really are. Too often we deceive ourselves into thinking we are pretty good girls. We need a deeper view of our sin. We were dead in our trespasses and sins, walking according to Satan's ways, fulfilling our fleshly desires, and under God's wrath (Eph. 2:1–3). We were not good little girls with clean hands and pretty dresses whom the Father couldn't wait to have in His family. Instead, we were unclean, filthy, unholy, and completely unworthy to stand in the presence of God. As those who have been saved by grace alone through faith alone, we should recognize the gift we have been given and live in light of the truth that we are heirs with Christ. We should submit ourselves to Him, pouring out our time, talents, and treasures for the sake of Jesus.

Oftentimes we forget that Jesus wants our love. Isn't it amazing that Jesus acknowledged this great act of love by this woman and defended her lavishness? Mary never thought about what the sacrificial gift cost her because Mary was driven by love. Is that true for you and me? Our world has cheapened the definition of love by exchanging it for lust. The Word of God defines love differently. According to Scripture, love is an action. By keeping God's Word we show our great love for Him (1 John 2:5–6). He must be both Lord and Savior of our lives. And by loving our neighbor we show how much we love God (1 John 2:9–11). Jesus said, "A new commandment I give to you, that you love one another; as I have loved you, that you also love one another. By this all will know that you are My disciples, if you have love for one another" (John 13:34–35). Our covenant relationship with God places us in a covenant relationship with His people. We can't say we love God and refuse to have anything to do with His people. We can't say we love Christ and not love His church.

I have had this conversation with my older children. A good barometer of our relationship with God is not how often we read our Bible or pray or attend church, although those things are extremely important, but how much we love those in our home, extended family, neighborhood, and other spheres of influence. This is a good test for me as well. If I'm biting and devouring my husband and children by any of my words or actions, it doesn't matter how much time I'm spending in my study reading God's Word and praying or how many Bible studies I'm teaching. My attitudes and actions show that I do not love God if I do not show love to my husband and children. Ouch! Is this as convicting for you as it is for me?

We tend to draw a dichotomy where Scripture brings unity. Our relationship with others flows from our relationship with God. If things aren't going well in our relationships, it's likely that something is amiss in our relationship with the Lord. For example, if I am angry with my husband because he does not want to move and I do, my anger is ultimately toward God. Since He is the one in control of my circumstances, and He gave me my husband as my authority, I must first come to terms with His sovereignty and providence over my situation and submit my desires to Him. You may not want to move, but you may be ready to get engaged, and your boyfriend is not; or you may be ready to have children, and your husband is not; or you may be ready for a promotion at work, but your supervisor hasn't offered the position to you. Regardless, the way we respond to others is a barometer of our love for the Lord.

Mary Chooses the Good Portion

We glorify God not just by loving Him but also by enjoying Him. In Luke 10:38–42 we learn that Jesus entered the village where Mary and Martha lived. Martha welcomed Jesus into her home. Martha's sister, Mary, sat at Jesus's feet and heard His words. But Martha was distracted with the needs of serving. She went to Jesus and questioned whether He cared that she was serving alone while her sister sat at His feet. Then she told Jesus to tell Mary to help her. Jesus replied, "Martha, Martha, you are worried and troubled about many things. But one thing is needed, and Mary has chosen that good part, which will not be taken away from her" (Luke 10:41–42). There are several significant things to note in this story.

First, Mary sat and listened to Jesus teaching. No doubt Mary had many other things she could have been doing. We certainly know that Martha thought so! But Mary enjoyed Jesus's company and Jesus's teaching so much that she sat down and listened. This is how we enjoy God. We sit down and listen to His teaching through the Word of God. We spend time with Him. We put aside other things, even pressing things, in order to enjoy time with Him in prayer and the Word. We don't just do this alone. We go to church on Sunday and sit among God's people. We listen to the preaching of God's Word, putting aside other things we could be doing on a Sunday morning and Sunday evening in order to hear from Jesus.

Second, Mary was not distracted by much serving. It is a fact that service can be a great distraction from one's relationship with the Lord. Although I don't want to draw a stark dichotomy between enjoying God and serving Him, there is a difference. I serve Him when I go and teach a Bible study. I enjoy Him when I stop, say no to all other duties, and spend time in prayer and reading His Word. I serve Him when I leave my home and family, fly to another country, and proclaim the gospel at a women's conference. I enjoy Him when I sing praises to Him in the midst of God's people at that same conference or in corporate worship. I serve Him when I disciple the four children He has given me according to His Word. I enjoy Him when I reflect on His good creation on an evening walk and praise Him for it.

Third, Mary left Martha to serve alone. Now wait a minute. You may think it's never okay to leave someone to serve alone. But here we see that Jesus commends Mary for saying no to service, no to helping someone who wants her help, and yes to Him. And if you and I want to enjoy God, we are going to have to say no to serving sometimes in order to be with Him. The problem is that the need for serving often screams at us, while the need for enjoying God's presence is often a quiet whisper. We get a flood of emails, text messages, or social media posts requesting our service. But never does JesusChrist@gmail.com appear in our inbox requesting us to sit at His feet. Yet it is in His presence that we find joy. As David says,

> You will show me the path of life;
> In Your presence is fullness of joy;
> At Your right hand are pleasures forevermore.
> (Ps. 16:11)

Fourth, Mary was not anxious and troubled about many things. She was able to enjoy her time with the Lord because she wasn't anxious and troubled about serving. Instead, she was awed with the teaching of the Almighty. So much so that she was compelled to stay seated. When we devote our time to studying Scripture, we will be compelled to stay seated. The more rooted we are in God's Word, the less we'll be uprooted by the fears of our flesh. Our fear will give way to recognition of God's faithfulness. Our anxious thoughts will give way to thoughts of the Almighty God. Our depression will give way to the delights of His Word. And our control will submit to the One who controls all things by His sovereign hand.

Fifth, Mary chose the good portion, which would never be taken from her. Mary chose to enjoy a relationship with Jesus before she chose to serve in Jesus's name. It is my strong conviction that service must flow from seated women. When we are not seated before the Lord, listening to His teaching by studying His Word and communicating with Him in prayer, we will have nothing to offer those we minister to that is worthy of Jesus's name. We may be able to fool those we serve for a time. But after a while our tanks will become empty and we'll burn out. The key to finishing well in the service of Christ is finding time to sit at His feet each and every day, refueling our tanks before serving in His name.

❖ ❖ ❖ ❖

When I looked closely at what was going on in my marriage and family life, I realized that it was connected to what was going on with my relationship with the Lord. I had forgotten that He had created each one of these people in my home intricately and wonderfully. I had ignored the fact that all of us are sinners, most especially me, and I could not yet expect the perfect marriage and family life. I had forgotten the power of redemption. Christ had begun a good work in all of us, and He would not fail to complete it. I was ignoring His sovereignty in bringing us all together as one family, sometimes wondering whether bringing these six people together was such a good idea. And I too often took my eyes off eternity, when we will be glorified. In other words, my faith in what God was doing as Creator and Redeemer was very weak. On the days when my love for my family grows colder instead of warmer, I need to check my relationship with the Lord. Am I recognizing His love for me and loving Him in return? Do I recognize that He enjoys being with His people, and am I in return enjoying being with Him and His people? Do I recognize Him as Creator and Redeemer? Do you?

Thinking It Through

1. How do your love for and enjoyment with your family ebb and flow? How is this connected to your relationship with the Lord?

2. How does Mary's affection for Jesus convict you or challenge you in your relationship with Him?

3. In what ways do you prioritize serving the Lord over sitting at His feet and listening to Him through His Word?

4. Have you ever considered the fact that we are to enjoy God? According to Scripture, what does it mean to enjoy Him (see, for example, Ps. 16:5–11)?

5. In speaking with a friend who has questions about the Christian faith, how could you use Mary's actions and Christ's response to help her understand what it means to have a relationship with Christ?

6. Do you weigh what you do for the gospel by what it's going to cost you, or do you give yourself unreservedly to Christ and His church? Spend time in prayer, repenting of any sin and asking the Lord to enable you to give yourself unreservedly to Christ and His church.

7. How does your church family help you love God and enjoy Him? How do you help others in your church family love and enjoy God?

8. Seek to memorize 1 John 3:16.

Chapter 9

Trusting and Obeying God

If you're a mom, you have probably said to your children "Just trust me," or "You need to obey me" more times than you can count. If you're not a mom, I'm sure you can remember your mom or dad saying these words to you. We say these words because we love our children and oftentimes have far greater wisdom than they do. So when they're about to make a bad decision, we often say "Trust me, and thank me later!" Or when they're about to disobey us, we command, "Obey me!" As we learned in our last chapter, our heavenly Father loves us. In fact, He enjoys being in relationship with us. Because He loves and enjoys us, we glorify God by loving Him and enjoying Him. In this chapter we will learn that our heavenly Father loves us so much that He also wants us to trust Him and obey Him.

God Is Trustworthy
It will be helpful to begin by recognizing that God is trustworthy. His faithfulness is rooted in His covenant. He has initiated a relationship with His people. This relationship does not depend upon our faithfulness

but His, and it is secured by the blood of His Son, Jesus Christ. After the Lord had made a covenant with David, David responded in humble thanksgiving. In the midst of his prayer he said, "You are God, and Your words are true, and You have promised this goodness to Your servant" (2 Sam. 7:28). This truth of God's trustworthiness is repeated several times in the psalms (Pss. 19:7; 111:7; 119:86, 138). It's not just in certain verses scattered through Scripture that we see God's faithfulness, though. We see His trustworthiness as the history of salvation unfolds from Genesis through Revelation. In the entirety of the covenantal structure of Scripture, we learn that God is faithful to fulfill His promises. As Paul says, "For all the promises of God in [Christ] are Yes, and in Him Amen" (2 Cor. 1:20). Because God has been faithful to us and saved us, we can trust Him by the power of the Holy Spirit. What does this trust look like in the life of the believer?

Mary's Trust in the Face of Fear

In Luke 1:26–38 we learn that God sent the angel Gabriel to Nazareth (a city of Galilee) to a virgin named Mary, who was engaged to a man named Joseph, of the line of David. The angel told Mary, "Rejoice, highly favored one, the Lord is with you; blessed are you among women!" (1:28). Mary was very troubled by the angel's saying and pondered what kind of greeting this was. However, the angel instructed her not to fear because she had found favor with God. She would have a son, and this son was to be named Jesus. The angel told her that Jesus would be great and called the Son of the Highest. The Lord

God would give Him the throne of His father David. He would reign forever in an eternal kingdom. Mary questioned how this could be, since she had never had sexual relations with a man. The angel told her that the Holy Spirit would come upon her and that by God's power she would conceive. The child she would carry would be called the Son of God. What is impossible for humans to accomplish is possible for God to bring about. Mary replied to the angel, "Behold the maidservant of the Lord! Let it be to me according to your word" (1:38).

We can learn a lot about what it means to trust the Lord from this passage. First, when Mary had every reason to fear, she responded in faith. She trusted the Lord as her King and trusted His plans for her life. Think about the last time you were gripped with fear. Perhaps you were getting more serious in your relationship with a man, and you weren't sure if you wanted to open up your heart to possibly be broken. Or maybe the career path you had chosen wasn't going as you had expected, and you feared the outcome. Perhaps you, or a loved one, received a diagnosis that was difficult to hear and that drastically changed your lifestyle. Maybe you were headed on vacation and feared for your family's safety, especially your young children's. Perhaps you were afraid about how the difficulties in your marriage were going to turn out. Or maybe you feared your teenager being rejected by his or her peers. Perhaps you feared your parents' aging process and the level of care they required. Or maybe you feared a hurricane that was projected to devastate your city.

Whatever triggers it, and whenever it comes, fear is no fun. It paralyzes us by stealing our faith so that we falter in trusting God's faithfulness. Instead of trusting the King, we question His kingdom purposes and wind up flailing our arms in fear instead of fighting fear with faith. The cure is a return to recognizing who God is. He is almighty, beloved, eternal, exalted, faithful, good, holy, immortal, mighty, omnipotent, undefiled, and victorious. He is the Creator, Defender, Joy, King, Lord, Name above all names, Prince of Peace, Leader beside quiet waters, Restorer, Savior, Truth, Wonderful Counselor, Yahweh (Covenant Keeper), and the One who reigns from the heavenly Zion. When we recognize who He is, we will trust His plans for our life.

Second, Mary's trust was grounded in the truth of Scripture. Her song of praise in Luke 1:46–55 echoes Hannah's in 1 Samuel 2. She recognized that God is magnificent, merciful, gracious, mighty, great, holy, and strong in power. She worshiped Him as the Savior, Helper, and Covenant Keeper. She recognized that God has been faithful to His people throughout the ages. Just as He had been faithful to Hannah, so He would be faithful to her. Just as He had been faithful to Israel, so He would fulfill His words to her.

We don't trust a God we don't know. He has revealed Himself through His Word and His works, giving us every reason to trust Him. The same God who spoke creation into existence, formed you in your mother's womb, stilled the raging storm, raised Lazarus from the dead, and raised Himself from the dead is the God who is sovereign over all the events of our lives.

Trust for the believer is turning from the temptation to drink from broken cisterns to Jesus, the author and finisher of our faith (Heb. 12:2). Trust recognizes that our heavenly Father has the best plan for our lives. Trust understands that this plan isn't going to go according to our plan. Trust is satisfied when our heavenly Father says no, or wait, to something we wanted. And trust takes Him at His word, believing His promises.

The prayer of trust is the prayer of 2 Chronicles 20:12: "For we have no power against this great multitude that is coming against us; nor do we know what to do, but our eyes are upon You." I prayed this prayer one night in my study when I didn't know what to do in a relational difficulty. As tears stung my eyes, trust took root in my heart. I felt as though a great multitude of problems surrounded me that were too deep for me to solve. And I had no idea where to even begin. But I took great comfort in knowing I could trust the Lord, so I looked to Him. This kind of trust doesn't mean that the letter denying you entrance into your top choice of graduate schools, or another dispute with your husband, or the road of infertility, or a life of chronic pain, or raising children, or caring for aging parents will be easy. And you may still have to walk through the valley of the shadow of death. But in the midst of the hardships, you have an anchor in the Word of God that will keep you steadfast in the faith. Immerse yourself in Scripture. We can't trust a God we don't know, and we can't know God apart from His Word. Let's eagerly pray that the God of hope will fill us with joy and peace as we trust in Him, that we might abound in hope by the Holy Spirit's power (Rom. 15:13).

Obeying God

Not only do we glorify God by loving Him, enjoying Him, and trusting Him. We also glorify God by obeying Him. As we noted earlier, these four things can't be separated from one another. For example, Jesus says, "If you love Me, keep My commandments" (John 14:15). Thankfully, Jesus relieves any anxious thoughts about how we can do this by immediately saying, "And I will pray the Father, and He will give you another Helper, that He may abide with you forever" (14:16). It is the Holy Spirit who enables us to obey. So let's take a look at what it means to walk by the Spirit so that we can obey God.

Crucified with Christ

Sometime soon, consider reading the entire book of Galatians out loud. If you're studying this book with a group, consider reading it out loud together. When you do this, you will likely be struck by how serious a letter it is. Nothing less than the gospel is at stake. There is a battle raging between the true gospel and a false gospel, and Paul has to address it. It's unlikely that you're on vacation at the beach right now, although you might be! Instead, you're probably in the midst of relationships that seem ruined, suffering that seems to be strangling your soul, sin that seems to be swallowing you whole, and service that seems too stressful to continue. Instead of flip-flops and a towel, you need armor. You need to know how to fight the battle we're in against the world, the flesh, and the devil.

In Galatians 2:20–21 Paul makes it clear that believers have been crucified with Christ. This means that

Christ lives in us through His Spirit. Not only this, but we live by faith in Christ, who loved us and gave Himself for us. Righteousness comes through Christ. It is the grace of God that saves us and sanctifies us. So we never move past the gospel in the Christian life. This is important to remember when we speak about walking in the Spirit.

Walk by the Spirit

In Galatians 5:16–26 Paul tells us that if we walk in the Spirit we won't fulfill our fleshly lusts. The flesh and the Spirit of God are at war within us. Paul tells us that these fleshly works that wage war within our hearts are evident in our actions. Actions such as "adultery, fornication, uncleanness, lewdness, idolatry, sorcery, hatred, contentions, jealousies, outbursts of wrath, selfish ambitions, dissensions, heresies, envy, murders, drunkenness, revelries, and the like" (5:19–21). Paul says that those who practice these things will not inherit the kingdom of God. On the other hand, "the fruit of the Spirit is love, joy, peace, longsuffering, kindness, goodness, faithfulness, gentleness, self-control" (5:22–23). As those who are Christ's, our fleshly passions and desires are crucified. We already live in the Spirit. But Paul says we must walk in the Spirit too. We must strive to "not become conceited, provoking one another, envying one another" (5:26).

We should note several important truths in these verses. First, if we walk by the Spirit, we will not gratify the desires of the flesh. We cannot do both at the same time. We can either walk by the flesh, thereby grieving the Spirit of God, or we can walk by the Spirit and not gratify the flesh.

Second, because the desires of the flesh are against the Spirit, and the desires of the Spirit are against the flesh, we can want to do what is right and still do what is wrong. This is why there are times when we don't do the things we want to do as a believer. For example, have you ever been in an argument with someone and really wanted to stop, but you kept sinning, saying things you shouldn't have said? Later, you might have even reflected on that event and recalled how strong your fleshly lusts had been in the heat of the moment. As new creatures in Christ, we don't have to sin, but since our flesh is still alive and well on this side of glory, we can and will still sin. Knowing this is crucial because we won't be surprised when war comes, and we will be equipped for battle.

Third, the works of the flesh that Paul lists describe who we are apart from the intervention of God in our lives. But even as believers, we still battle the temptation toward each one of these things. We have to strive against them, especially when our flesh craves them and when the world and the devil hold them out to us dressed up in dazzling colors to lure us into thinking they are the solution to our dissatisfaction. For example, sexual immorality is dressed up in our culture on the front cover of magazines that define beauty as sexy. Drunkenness is dressed up as a cool drink to relax from the stresses of life. And idolatry is dressed up in media and games that have stolen time and energy from our families and wreaked havoc in our hearts and minds.

Fourth, there is a serious warning. Paul warns his readers that those who are characterized by the works of the flesh will not inherit the kingdom of God. This warning is intended to lead us to repentance, and it should convict us to pray for those we know who are involved in such things, asking the Lord to bring them to repentance and then knowledge of the truth, so they may escape the trap Satan has them in (2 Tim. 2:25–26).

Fifth, in stark contrast to the works of the flesh, Paul talks about the fruit of the Spirit. Most of us are so familiar with this list that it's become something we can easily rattle off or sing, but all too often when we are picked (if we can compare ourselves to a fruit tree for a moment), this is not what we produce.

As we look at each one of these characteristics, keep in mind that this fruit in our lives does not come about by just letting go and letting God have His way with us. Neither does it come about by willpower, as though we could will ourselves to be Spirit-filled women. Instead, we strive for these characteristics, knowing that it is the Holy Spirit who enables us to bear such fruit. One of my daily prayers comes from the Heidelberg Catechism:

> By ourselves we are too weak to hold our own even for a moment. And our sworn enemies—the devil, the world, and our own flesh, never stop attacking us. And so, Lord, uphold us and make us strong with the strength of Your Holy Spirit, so that we may not go down to defeat in this spiritual struggle, but may firmly resist our enemies until we finally win the complete victory (A. 127).

The Fruit of the Spirit
It's common to hear people list the fruit of the Spirit, but not as common to hear them define it. So I want

to unpack what each of these words (love, joy, peace, patience, kindness, goodness, faithfulness, gentleness, and self-control) means. First, in 1 John 4:7–21 we learn that love is from God. In fact, God is love. He displayed His love by sending Christ to atone for our sins. Our love for one another comes from God abiding in us. In other words, we love because God first loved us. If we love God, then we will love one another. Love can't be separated from the other qualities mentioned. This is because God's love in us is necessary for all the other qualities to be present in our lives.

Second, the joy of the Lord is our strength (Neh. 8:10). We don't gain joy from circumstances but from a heart that beats for the things of God. The Lord fills us with joy in His presence (Ps. 16:11). It is the Bridegroom, Jesus Christ, who gives us fullness of joy. This means that we can have joy even in the midst of great suffering or difficult service. If we gained joy from circumstances, our joy would ebb and flow from one moment to the next. But since our joy comes from God's presence, we can know joy as we abide in Christ.

Third, Christ is our peace. He has reconciled us to God and to one another. We must strive to be peacemakers because Christ first became a peacemaker between God and us. The reason we're not to let the sun go down on our anger (Eph. 4:26) is that Christ died so that we could be restored to God and to one another.

Fourth, God is displaying His patience as He delays Christ's second coming so that more and more people might be saved. He has the greater good in mind, and His plan and timing are perfect. We are to be patient because He has first been patient with us. This means that we should be longsuffering as we earnestly pray for God to save our loved ones. It means that we should be patient as we watch and wait for the Lord to sanctify our husband and children, or our friend and neighbor. We want others to be patient with us, and yet we are slow to extend patience to others. They get in the way of our comfort and convenience, and we oftentimes demand that they change. We must extend grace to them, waiting patiently for the Lord to bring about the fruit of the Spirit in their lives.

Fifth, God displays His kindness in order to lead sinners to repentance (Rom. 2:4). God's kindness is closely linked with His patience. It is kind that He is not quick to bring judgment but is merciful to us, giving us time to turn toward Him. We are to be kind also, not quick to judge but extending mercy to others. One evening there was a knock on my door. It was one of my friend's children. Earlier that day I had seen him at the grocery store with another friend of his whom I also knew. When our eyes met in the aisle, it seemed as though something was amiss, so I questioned whether his dad knew he was there. He looked me in the eye and told me his dad knew. I asked whether they needed anything (a ride home, for example), but they declined.

That evening I invited him into my kitchen. He confessed that he had lied to me and told me he was sorry. As I extended forgiveness to him, I shared with him a story from my childhood about a time I had stolen erasers that I really liked from my teacher's desk. They were fruit-shaped and scented, and I slowly filled my backpack full of them as the days went by. I told him that it was this incident in my life that had shown me for the first time that I was a sinner in need of a Savior. Guilt had eaten me up, and when I told my mom what I had done she drove me to confess my sin to the headmaster of the Christian school where the incident had occurred. As I shared now with this young man my own sinfulness, I could see his posture relax. Instead of reprimanding him, I received him as a fellow sinner in need of God's grace.

A few days later there was another knock on my door. It was his friend who had been with him at the grocery store. As she confessed that she had lied, I shared the same story about the erasers. A few days later she knocked on my door again and gave me a brand new package of fruit-scented erasers. I smiled and thanked her, recognizing that she was returning my kindness with a kindness of her own. She was thanking me for being merciful. I need to be merciful far more often than I am. It's easy to be impatient and unkind, especially with those we love the most. But the Lord has been merciful and kind to us, and He says we're to be the same to others.

Sixth, goodness is doing good to others because God has been good to us. Goodness is an action that benefits those around us, especially our brothers and sisters in Christ. We do good to others when we help them in need. They may be ill and in need of a meal. They might have a car issue and need a ride somewhere. They may need a free babysitter so they can get some errands done. They might need a bag of groceries during a difficult time financially. When we look around us we will see needs, and it is our job to fill them as we're able.

Seventh, God is faithful to His promises. This means that His Word is as good as done. We should be known for faithfulness as well. When we say we will do something, it should be as though it is already done. Dependability is a wonderful thing, yet it's often lacking in so many people today. Christians are to be loyal because Christ has been loyal to us.

Eighth, Jesus displays gentleness by inviting us to take His yoke upon us and learn from Him and to rest our souls in Him (Matt. 11:29). When others are around us, they should feel well rested in our presence, as though we have taken their burden from them to carry it for them. This is a wonderful gift to give someone when they come into your home with the headaches and heartaches of this world. You can point them to Jesus, encourage them to rest in Him, kneel with them in prayer, turn their eyes from the temporal to the eternal, love them with your words and actions, and encourage them with biblical truth.

Finally, it is only the Spirit that enables us to say no when our flesh wants to say yes. We must be self-controlled in saying no to everything Paul mentioned as a work of the flesh. In Scripture, self-control is connected with clear-mindedness, alertness, uprightness, godliness, purity, soundness in faith, and discipline. All these qualities are characteristics of soldiers. Soldiers must be clear-minded when they head into battle so that they can remember the battle plan. They must be alert to any attacks. They must be upright, godly, pure, and sound in the faith in order to be wise. And they must be disciplined to stay in good shape for the war. This may not sound as fun as wearing flip-flops on a sandy beach, but it's necessary if we're going to fight the flesh, the world, and the devil without experiencing defeat at every turn. We obey God when we walk by the Spirit and refuse to gratify the desires of the flesh. Such obedience produces the fruit of the Spirit in our lives. And this fruit glorifies God and enables us to enjoy Him forever.

The next time you say "Just trust me" to someone you love, remember that your heavenly Father loves you and wants you to love Him, enjoy Him, trust Him, and obey Him. If you're like Carol, whose trust and enjoyment were in social media instead of her Savior, and you're feeling depressed instead of delighting in your Deliverer, turn to Him today. If you're like Sarah, and you've turned to diet and exercise to fulfill you, turn again to Christ, who will never fail you. If you're like Gina, who tried to drown out her problems with compulsive shopping, run to your Redeemer, who has paid your debt and set you free from sin to live a life for His glory. If you're like Amy and are hooked on sexual sin and filled with shame inside, take your longings to Christ and let Him satisfy you instead. If you're like Lisa, filling your schedule to drown out the loneliness you feel inside, fill your head and heart with God's Word instead. If you're like Kay, fearing failure and focused on the next deadline, place your security in the shepherd of our souls. If you're like Tammy, pouring all your energies into your children and leaving no room for other relationships, recognize that your relationship with Christ must take first priority and that your relationship with His people is vitally important as well. If you have forsaken the Fountain of living waters in any way, and hewed out broken cisterns that can hold no water (and we all have), return to Him today in humble confession and adoration, drinking deeply of the water that He offers, which quenches our thirst for all eternity. Remember what Jesus told the Samaritan woman at the well: "Whoever drinks of the water that I shall give him will never thirst. But the water that I shall give him will become in him a fountain of water springing up into everlasting life" (John 4:14).

Thinking It Through

1. What did you learn about God's faithfulness in this chapter that you could apply to your present circumstances?

2. How could you use this knowledge of God's faithfulness to help someone having a hard time believing God can be trusted?

3. How did Mary trust God in the face of fear? How does this encourage you to trust the Lord with your fears?

4. What did you learn about the war in our hearts between the flesh and the Spirit? How did this help you better understand your present struggles?

5. What are some fleshly desires with which you are battling right now? How has this chapter encouraged you to continue fighting?

6. How have you seen the fruit of the Spirit grow in your life? What about in the lives of your children or husband, if they are saved? Take a moment this week to encourage one of your family members or friends regarding ways in which you see the fruit of the Spirit in his or her life.

7. Write out a prayer this week, asking the Lord to help you understand more of His faithfulness and to help you trust and obey Him more. Also pray this for your children, grandchildren, or the children in your church.

8. Seek to memorize John 14:15 this week.

9. Reflect on what you have learned in this book. Write down a few points that impacted you the most, and then consider sharing them with a friend or family member.

Bibliography

Carson, D. A. *The Gospel According to John.* The Pillar New Testament Commentary. Grand Rapids, MI: Eerdmans, 1991.

The Gospel Coalition and Redeemer Presbyterian Church. *The New City Catechism.* Wheaton, Ill.: Crossway, 2017.

House, Paul R. "Jeremiah." In ESV Study Bible: English Standard Version. Wheaton, Ill.: Crossway, 2008.

Ivill, Sarah. *The Covenantal Life: Appreciating the Beauty of Theology and Community.* Grand Rapids: Reformation Heritage Books, 2018.

———. *Ezra and Nehemiah: The Good Hand of Our God Is on Us.* Grand Rapids: Reformation Heritage Books, 2019.

———. *1 Peter, 2 Peter, and Jude: Steadfast in the Faith.* Grand Rapids: Reformation Heritage Books, 2017.

———. *Hebrews: His Hope: The Anchor for Our Souls.* Lawrenceville, Ga.: Christian Education and Publications, 2011.

———. *Judges and Ruth: There Is a Redeemer.* Phillipsburg, N.J.: P&R, 2014.

————. *Never Enough: Confronting Lies about Appearance and Achievement with Gospel Hope.* Grand Rapids: Reformation Heritage Books, 2019.

————. *Revelation: Let the One Who Is Thirsty Come.* Phillipsburg, N.J.: P&R, 2013.

————. *Romans: The Gospel of God for Obedience to the Faith.* Grand Rapids: Reformation Heritage Books, 2020.

The Orthodox Presbyterian Church. *The Westminster Confession of Faith and Catechisms,* as adopted by the Presbyterian Church in America with Proof Texts. Lawrenceville, Ga.: Christian Education and Publications, 2005, 2007.